PAT BROWN, MBA

Soccer Money 101

Using Soccer to Teach the Basics of Money

ABRAM 47 BROWN

First published by AbramBrown47 2026

First edition

ISBN: 978-1-967737-61-1

This book was professionally typeset on Reedsy.
Find out more at reedsy.com

Contents

Foreword v
Introduction viii
About This Book xii
Foolish Assumptions xvi
How This Playbook Is Organized xx
About Pat Brown xxiii
Part I: First Touch and Fundamentals (Preseason) 1
Chapter 1: Why Money Feels Confusing After Soccer 3
Chapter 2: See the Whole Pitch: Your Financial Snapshot 8
Chapter 3: Building Possession: Budgeting and Saving 13
Chapter 4: Playing With Borrowed Time: Credit and Debt 18
Chapter 5: The Clubhouse of Money: Banking Basics 24
Part II: Defensive Shape and Protection 30
Chapter 6: Risk Awareness and Decision Making 32
Chapter 7: Insurance Fundamentals Every Player Needs 37
Chapter 8: Life, Disability, and Liability Protection 43
Part III: Building the Attack (Investing Fundamentals) 48
Chapter 9: How the Financial Markets Really Work 50
Chapter 10: Risk, Return, and the Power of Compounding 55
Chapter 11: Stocks Without the Transfer Rumors 60
Chapter 12: Bonds and Controlling the Midfield 64
Chapter 13: Funds, ETFs, and Team-Based Investing 69
Chapter 14: Real Estate and Alternative Plays 74
Part IV: Managing the Match (Portfolio Management) 79
Chapter 15: Asset Allocation and Squad Selection 81
Chapter 16: Buying, Holding, and Trusting the System 86

Chapter 17: Halftime Adjustments and Rebalancing 91
Chapter 18: The Mental Side of Money 96
Part V: The Full Season and the Long Career 101
Chapter 19: Taxes and Where You Hold the Ball 103
Chapter 20: Retirement Accounts and Financial Independence 108
Chapter 21: Housing and Big Life Transfers 113
Chapter 22: Your Career Is Your Academy 118
Chapter 23: Estate Planning Basics Everyone Needs 123
Chapter 24: Talking About Money With Family 128
Part VI: Playing the Long Game 133
Chapter 25: Advisors, Scams, and Long-Term Success 135
Chapter 26: Losing the Schedule and Rebuilding Structure 141
Chapter 27: From Teammates to Coworkers 146
Chapter 28: When No One Is Watching Anymore 151
Chapter 29: Redefining Winning After the Uniform Comes Off 156
Chapter 30: Staying Connected Without Living in the Past 161
Glossary of Soccer and Financial Terms 167
Disclaimers 174

Foreword

Soccer teaches you things long before anyone ever sits you down to talk about money.

It teaches you patience. You cannot force the match when the moment is not there. You learn to move the ball, recycle possession, and wait for space to open. You learn that the best teams are not the ones sprinting nonstop, but the ones controlling tempo.

It teaches you discipline. Showing up late, skipping recovery, or drifting mentally gets exposed quickly. The game has a way of punishing shortcuts. You either respect the process, or the process finds you.

It teaches you accountability. There is no hiding on the pitch. Your positioning matters. Your decisions matter. Your effort matters. Teammates feel it immediately when you are not locked in.

What soccer rarely teaches you, however, is how those same lessons apply once the final whistle blows and the structure disappears.

For many players, life after soccer feels disorienting. The training schedule is gone. The coaching staff is gone. The matchday routine is gone. Suddenly, decisions that used to be made for you are now yours alone. No one is setting your calendar. No one is reviewing film with you. No one is correcting mistakes in real time.

Money often becomes the place where that lack of structure shows up first.

You earn income, but no one explains how to manage it. You hear advice from teammates, friends, social media, and locker room legends, but very little of it is grounded in fundamentals. One person swears by a shortcut. Another claims they got rich fast. Everyone seems confident. Almost no one shows you the full picture.

That is where many athletes lose possession.

They chase quick wins instead of building patiently. They confuse confidence with competence. They mistake activity for progress. They panic during downturns and force plays that do not need to be forced.

This book exists to change that.

Soccer Money 101 is not about turning athletes into financial experts. It is about giving you a familiar playbook for decisions you will face long after your playing days are over. The same principles that helped you compete on the field are the ones that build long-term financial strength off it.

Possession matters. You cannot control a match if you cannot control the ball. Financially, you cannot build stability if you do not understand where your money is going, how it moves, and why it behaves the way it does.

Discipline matters. Great teams stick to their shape even when emotions run high. In money, discipline shows up as saving consistently, investing patiently, and avoiding the temptation to chase every headline or trend.

Vision matters. The best players are not just reacting to what is in front of them. They are scanning the pitch, anticipating the next pass, and thinking two or three moves ahead. Financial success works the same way. Short-term decisions always feel louder than long-term ones, but long-term vision is what wins seasons, not moments.

This book uses soccer because soccer already taught you how to think this way.

You understand reps. You understand development. You understand that form comes and goes, but fundamentals endure. You know that one bad match does not define a season, and one great goal does not guarantee success.

Money works the same way.

There will be volatility. There will be setbacks. There will be moments where the crowd noise is loud and the pressure feels real. The goal is not to avoid mistakes entirely. The goal is to build a system that keeps small mistakes from becoming season-ending ones.

Throughout this book, you will see financial concepts explained through scenarios you recognize. Managing risk will feel like knowing when to press and when to drop. Diversification will feel like squad depth. Rebalancing will feel like halftime adjustments. Long-term investing will feel like trusting the training plan instead of chasing results after one bad week.

You do not need to be perfect to win the long game. You need to be consistent.

That is why this book avoids hype, shortcuts, and complicated jargon. It focuses on fundamentals, structure, and decision-making. It treats money like a season, not a highlight reel.

Soccer careers are often short. Financial lives are not.

Whether you played at the youth level, high school, college, or beyond, the transition away from the game can feel abrupt. But the habits soccer gave you are not gone. They are transferable. They just need a new field.

This book is your bridge.

It is designed to help you take the mindset that made you competitive and apply it to building stability, freedom, and confidence over time. Not overnight. Not through luck. Through preparation, discipline, and trust in the process.

Value the ball.

Control the tempo.

Play the long game.

The final whistle does not mean the lessons stop. It means they matter more than ever.

Introduction

The final whistle is one of the quietest loud moments in sports.

One second you are sprinting, tracking, competing, adjusting. The next, it is over. No huddle. No extra instructions. No clear next play. Just space where structure used to be.

For most soccer players, the end does not come with drama. It comes after the season. After graduation. After a contract does not renew. After priorities shift. One day you simply stop preparing for the next match.

Life moves on. You are expected to move with it.

This book exists because that transition is harder than most people admit.

When the Structure Disappears

Soccer gives you a framework for everything.

Your schedule is built. Your goals are defined. Your progress is measured. You know what a good day looks like. You know what you are training for.

When that structure disappears, life feels open at first. Then it feels unanchored.

Decisions multiply. No one tells you when to train, when to recover, or when to review film. There is no season to reset mistakes. There is no coach pushing accountability. Discipline becomes optional instead of enforced.

Money enters this vacuum quickly.

You are suddenly responsible for managing income, expenses, debt, taxes, savings, and long-term decisions with no playbook and no position coach. Most players are never trained for this part of the game.

Why Money Feels Different After Soccer

Money is not like the game.

There is no scoreboard. No immediate feedback. No film session that shows mistakes the next morning. Consequences show up later, sometimes years later.

That delay is dangerous.

Athletes are trained to respond to pressure and urgency. Money rewards patience and consistency. The skill sets overlap, but they are not identical.

This mismatch causes confusion.

Some former players take too much risk because confidence feels like tolerance. Others avoid decisions entirely because uncertainty feels uncomfortable. Many drift because nothing feels urgent enough to act on.

None of this means athletes are bad with money. It means they were never taught how to translate their strengths into this environment.

The Hidden Transition No One Talks About

The physical transition out of soccer is visible. The identity shift is talked about occasionally. The financial transition is often ignored.

Yet money touches everything that comes next.

Where you live. What jobs you take. How much stress you carry. How much freedom you have. How long options stay open.

Financial mistakes made early rarely show up right away. They compound quietly. By the time they are obvious, choices feel limited.

This book is meant to arrive before that point.

What This Book Is and Is Not

This is not a get-rich-quick book. It is not a prediction of markets. It is not a collection of hacks or shortcuts.

It is a translation.

It takes financial concepts and frames them through the language you already understand. Training. Reps. Game plans. Adjustments. Seasons. Long-term development.

The goal is not perfection. The goal is control.

Control over decisions. Control over risk. Control over direction.

Why Soccer Makes This Easier Than You Think

Soccer players already possess the traits money requires.

Discipline. Patience. Conditioning. Long-term thinking. Comfort with repetition. Respect for fundamentals.

You learned that you cannot skip training and expect results. You learned that small mistakes compound over a match. You learned that preparation shows up when pressure rises.

Those lessons apply directly to finances.

The challenge is not ability. It is translation.

The New Match

Life after the final whistle is not empty. It is different.

There is no season schedule, but there is a long horizon. There is no coach, but there is still accountability. There is no match day, but there are daily decisions that matter just as much.

Money is part of that new match.

Handled well, it creates freedom, stability, and options. Handled poorly, it creates stress, limitation, and regret.

This book is your new playbook.

Not for one season, but for the decades that follow.

Athlete Takeaways

- The end of soccer removes structure, not responsibility.
- Money feels harder because feedback is delayed, not because you lack ability.

- Financial success is about translation, not talent.
- The discipline that built your game can build your future too.

About This Book

This book is built on a simple idea.

You already know how to succeed. You just have not been shown how those skills apply to money.

Soccer taught you far more than tactics and technique. It taught you how progress actually works. Through repetition. Through patience. Through discipline. Through long-term thinking. Those same principles drive financial success, even though the environment looks completely different.

The challenge is translation.

Why Traditional Money Advice Misses Athletes

Most personal finance advice is written for people who did not grow up in structured, competitive environments.

It assumes motivation problems instead of discipline gaps. It relies on abstract concepts instead of lived experience. It explains what to do without connecting to how athletes already think and learn.

As a result, athletes often tune out.

Not because the information is wrong, but because it is presented in a language that does not resonate.

This book does not ask you to become someone else to manage money well. It shows you how to apply what you already know.

Soccer Is a Long-Term Game

Soccer rewards patience.

You do not win matches in the first five minutes. You build possession. You control tempo. You manage energy. You wait for the right moments.

Money works the same way.

There are moments to attack, moments to protect, and moments to hold shape. Success comes from understanding timing, not forcing plays.

Trying to rush financial outcomes usually creates mistakes. The discipline you learned on the pitch is designed for this environment.

Fundamentals Win Seasons

Every coach preaches fundamentals.

First touch. Passing accuracy. Positioning. Conditioning. These are not exciting, but they decide matches.

Financial fundamentals work the same way.

Budgeting. Saving. Managing debt. Protecting downside. Investing consistently. These habits are not flashy, but they control outcomes.

This book emphasizes fundamentals first because advanced strategies fail without them.

You cannot skip steps and expect control.

Training, Reps, and Consistency

You did not become competent by accident.

You trained. You repeated drills. You stacked good days. You trusted that progress would show up later.

Financial success follows the same pattern.

Small, consistent actions matter more than intensity. Automating habits works better than relying on motivation. Systems outperform willpower.

This book is designed to help you build routines, not chase moments.

Risk, Confidence, and Decision-Making

Athletes are comfortable with pressure.

That confidence can be a strength or a liability with money. Emotional confidence does not always match financial capacity.

Soccer teaches situational awareness. Knowing when to press and when to drop. Knowing when to take a risk and when to protect shape.

Financial decisions require the same awareness.

This book separates emotional comfort from actual risk so decisions fit your real situation, not just your mindset.

Coaches, Systems, and Accountability

No athlete develops alone.

Coaches provide structure. Systems create consistency. Accountability keeps standards high.

Money requires the same support.

This book encourages building systems that enforce discipline even when life gets busy. It also explains when and how to seek guidance without giving up control.

Accountability does not disappear when sports end. It just changes form.

Seasons, Adjustments, and the Long View

Soccer careers are built over seasons.

You adjust roles. You adapt to injuries. You respond to competition. You evolve.

Financial lives work the same way.

Income changes. Goals shift. Families grow. Markets move. The plan must adjust without panic.

This book is structured like a season, moving from fundamentals to protection, growth, management, and long-term success.

What You Will Gain From This Approach

By the end of this book, you will not just know more about money. You will think about it differently.

You will see financial decisions as part of a long match, not isolated moments. You will understand how to control risk instead of reacting to it. You will build habits that work quietly over time.

Most importantly, you will stop feeling behind.

You are not starting from zero. You are translating existing skills into a new arena.

Foolish Assumptions

Every book makes assumptions.

Some of them are helpful. Some of them are foolish. The problem is that most money books never tell you what they assume about you. They just talk past your experience and wonder why it does not land.

This section makes the assumptions explicit.

If these assumptions do not fit you perfectly, that is fine. They are not requirements. They are starting points.

Assumption One: You Understand Discipline Better Than Most People

This book assumes you know what discipline actually is.

Not motivation. Not hype. Not wanting something badly. Discipline as showing up when it is boring, repetitive, and uncomfortable.

You trained when tired. You practiced fundamentals you already "knew." You followed plans that did not pay off immediately.

That matters.

Many people struggle with money because they have never practiced delayed gratification. You have.

If you applied discipline in sports, you can apply it financially. The issue is not capacity. It is translation.

Assumption Two: You Are Comfortable With Structure, Even If You Miss It

This book assumes structure does not scare you.

You lived inside schedules, systems, and expectations for years. You know that freedom does not come from chaos. It comes from preparation.

Money requires structure.

Budgets. Systems. Rules. Boundaries. These are not restrictions. They are the framework that allows flexibility later.

If you resist structure now, it is likely because it is no longer provided automatically, not because it does not work.

Assumption Three: You Have Felt Pressure and Performed Anyway

This book assumes you have operated under pressure.

You have made decisions while tired. You have competed with stakes. You have recovered from mistakes in real time.

That experience matters.

Money creates a different kind of pressure. Quieter. Slower. Less visible. But the same emotional responses show up.

If you have learned to stay composed in matches, you can learn to stay composed in financial decisions.

Assumption Four: You Respect Fundamentals, Even When They Are Boring

This book assumes you do not need flash to stay engaged.

You understand that fundamentals win games. That the best players do simple things extremely well. That shortcuts usually show up on film later.

Financial fundamentals are no different.

Saving. Budgeting. Managing debt. Diversifying. Reviewing plans. None of it is exciting. All of it works.

If you trust fundamentals in sports, you can trust them with money.

Assumption Five: You Are More Coachable Than You Realize

This book assumes you are coachable.

Not in the sense of being passive, but in the sense of being willing to learn, adjust, and apply feedback.

Athletes understand that improvement requires openness. Money is no different.

If you are willing to question assumptions, revisit habits, and make small adjustments, progress follows.

Assumption Six: You Care About the Long Game

This book assumes you care about more than short-term wins.

You trained for seasons, not moments. You accepted that progress was uneven. You stayed committed through setbacks.

Financial success requires the same mindset.

If you only focus on quick results, money becomes stressful. If you focus on long-term development, it becomes manageable.

Assumption Seven: You Are a Person First, Not Just a Former Player

This book assumes you are not defined solely by soccer.

Your identity is larger than your position, your minutes, or your stats. You have values, relationships, and goals beyond the game.

Money should support that life, not replace it.

If finances start driving identity instead of serving it, something is off.

Why These Assumptions Matter

These assumptions shape how this book is written.

It does not talk down to you. It does not oversimplify effort. It does not rely on hype or fear.

It assumes you can handle responsibility, nuance, and long-term thinking.

If that feels accurate, this book will resonate.

If it does not, take what applies and leave the rest.

How This Playbook Is Organized

This book is organized the same way a season is built.

You do not start with advanced tactics. You do not jump straight into attacking schemes. You begin with fundamentals, build structure, add protection, develop the attack, manage the match, and finish with long-term durability.

Each part builds on the one before it.

You can read this book cover to cover, or you can jump to the section that matches where you are right now. The structure is designed to work either way.

Preseason: First Touch and Fundamentals

The early chapters focus on control.

Cash flow. Budgeting. Saving. Debt. Banking. These topics may feel basic, but they decide everything that follows.

Just like first touch and positioning determine how fast you can play, financial fundamentals determine how much flexibility you have later.

If fundamentals are shaky, advanced strategies create more stress, not better outcomes.

Defensive Shape and Protection

Once fundamentals are in place, the focus shifts to protection.

Risk awareness. Insurance. Safeguards. This section is about preventing small problems from becoming season-ending setbacks.

In soccer, clean sheets come from discipline and positioning. Financially, protection creates stability so progress is not wiped out by one mistake or one event.

Building the Attack: Investing Fundamentals

With control and protection established, the book moves into growth.

This is where investing concepts are introduced. How markets work. Risk and return. Stocks, bonds, funds, and real estate.

The emphasis is on understanding, not hype.

Goals come from buildup, not desperation shots. Investing works best when it is patient, diversified, and consistent.

Managing the Match: Portfolio Management

Investing does not end once accounts are opened.

This section focuses on management. Asset allocation. Rebalancing. Emotional discipline. Adjustments as life changes.

Winning requires calm decisions, not panic substitutions. This part teaches how to review, adjust, and stay composed over time.

The Full Season and the Long Career

As the horizon extends, the focus shifts again.

Taxes. Retirement. Housing. Career decisions. Family conversations. Estate planning.

These chapters recognize that financial lives are long and interconnected. Decisions in one area affect others. Planning must account for multiple seasons, not just the next match.

Playing the Long Game

The final section brings everything together.

Choosing advisors wisely. Avoiding scams. Understanding long-term success. Rebuilding identity and structure after sports.

This is about durability. Protecting progress. Staying disciplined when no one is watching.

How to Use This Book

You can read straight through, or you can treat this like a playbook.

If money feels overwhelming, start with fundamentals.

If you are worried about risk, focus on protection.

If you want growth, study the investing sections.

If life is changing, revisit the long-term chapters.

There is no single correct path through the book. The right path is the one that matches your current season.

About Pat Brown

Pat Brown understands transition because he has lived it.

He played college football at the University of Kansas from 1994 to 1999 and was named team captain for the 1999 season. His years in the locker room shaped his views on accountability, discipline, preparation, and leadership. Those principles continue to guide his work long after football.

After his playing career, Pat transitioned into financial services and built a career as a financial advisor and private wealth manager. He works with individuals, families, business owners, and athletes navigating increasingly complex financial lives. His work spans financial planning, retirement income strategies, tax planning, and philanthropic planning, always with an emphasis on long-term clarity rather than short-term noise.

Pat pursued advanced education alongside real-world experience, earning an MBA and professional designations including ChFC®, RICP®, and CAP®. His approach blends structured planning with practical execution, grounded in the belief that fundamentals matter more than hype.

As the college sports landscape changed with the introduction of Name, Image, and Likeness opportunities, Pat recognized a growing education gap. Student-athletes were gaining access to income, contracts, and endorsements without the financial knowledge required to manage taxes, cash flow, business structures, and long-term consequences. That gap became the catalyst for his work in athlete financial education.

Pat has since become a recognized voice in this space and has been interviewed by national publications and platforms including Financial Planning, Yahoo, and ESPN Andscape. In those conversations, he focuses on financial literacy gaps, NIL planning challenges, and the realities facing athletes and their families during and after competition.

These experiences led Pat to author a series of athlete-focused books designed to meet readers where they are. His NIL-related titles include *Financial Literacy for NIL, Financial Literacy for NIL for Parents of Student Athletes, Financial Literacy for NIL for High School Students,* and *Financial Literacy for NIL for International Student Athletes.* Each book emphasizes clarity, discipline, and real-world application over theory.

Pat also created a growing collection of sport-specific financial education titles, including *Football Money 101, Baseball Money 101, Basketball Money 101, Cheer Money 101, Dance Money 101, Gymnastics Money 101, Hockey Money 101, Lacrosse Money 101, Rowing Money 101, Soccer Money 101, Softball Money 101, Tennis Money 101, Track Money 101, Volleyball Money 101,* and *Wrestling Money 101.* Each book translates the culture, discipline, and mindset of the sport into financial lessons athletes can apply long after competition ends.

To extend this mission beyond books, Pat founded Former Student Athlete, a platform created to support athletes navigating life after sports. The platform focuses on financial literacy, career transitions, health, identity, and long-term success once the uniform comes off. You can explore this work at www.formerstudentathlete.com, www.financialliteracyfornil.com, and www.financialliteracyforstudentathletes.com.

Pat is easy to find through a Google search, on LinkedIn, or on Twitter, where he regularly shares insights on athletes, money, and life after sports.

His work is rooted in a simple belief shaped by both football and finance. Athletes deserve a better playbook for life after sports, and financial education should arrive before opportunity turns into regret.

Part I: First Touch and Fundamentals (Preseason)

You cannot control the match if you cannot control the ball.

Every coach starts the same way.

Before tactics. Before formations. Before opponent scouting. The focus is on first touch, balance, and fundamentals. If you cannot receive the ball cleanly, everything else breaks down. Decision-making gets rushed. Confidence drops. The game speeds up.

Money works the same way.

Most financial stress does not come from complex strategies or bad luck. It comes from poor fundamentals. Not knowing where money is going. Not having margin. Not understanding basic tools. When the fundamentals are shaky, every decision feels urgent and emotional.

This section is your preseason.

It is about building control before pressure arrives. Understanding cash flow. Learning how to budget and save. Managing debt. Setting up basic banking systems. These are not advanced topics, but they are decisive ones.

Athletes often want to skip this part. Fundamentals feel boring. They do not feel impressive. But every great player knows that mastery shows up in the basics.

You cannot play fast if your touch is poor.

You cannot play smart if you are always scrambling.

You cannot attack if you are constantly defending mistakes.

Financial first touch gives you time and options. It slows the game down.

It allows you to make decisions instead of reacting to them.

This part of the book is not about restriction. It is about control.

Once fundamentals are solid, everything else becomes easier. Risk makes sense. Investing feels manageable. Long-term planning becomes possible.

Preseason is where seasons are won quietly.

Get the fundamentals right, and the rest of the match opens up.

Chapter 1: Why Money Feels Confusing After Soccer

Every soccer player knows the feeling of stepping into a match where the tempo is chaotic.

The ball is flying around. Both teams are pressing. Space is tight. Someone tries to force a killer pass that is not there. Possession gets turned over. Momentum swings. Suddenly, the game feels out of control.

Good teams respond by slowing things down. They recycle possession. They move the ball side to side. They trust the shape. They let the game come back to them.

Money feels confusing after soccer for the same reason a frantic match feels confusing. There is no structure. No clear system. Too much noise. Too many people shouting instructions at once.

When you played, you always knew the game plan. Even if you did not love it, there was a plan. Training followed a rhythm. Decisions were coached. Mistakes were corrected quickly.

With money, that structure often disappears overnight.

Why Financial Literacy Is Rarely Taught to Players

Most players never receive formal financial education because it was never part of the development pipeline.

Youth soccer focuses on touch, movement, and fundamentals. High school soccer adds competition and exposure. College and elite levels demand performance, results, and survival. At no point is there a built-in moment where someone sits you down and explains taxes, investing, or long-term planning.

The assumption is simple. You will figure it out later.

The problem is that later often shows up with real consequences. Bills. Contracts. Scholarships. Income swings. Injuries. Career transitions. Suddenly, money matters, and there is no coach explaining the system.

Another reason financial literacy is missing is that players are used to being told what to do. Training times are posted. Film is reviewed. Nutrition plans are handed out. When that guidance goes away, players are left making decisions without reps.

Money is no different than soccer. If you never practiced it, why would you expect to perform well under pressure?

Common Money Myths Passed Through the Locker Room

In every locker room, there is unofficial advice.

Someone always knows a guy. Someone swears a teammate made a fortune doing something fast. Someone else says saving is pointless because inflation eats it anyway. Another claims investing is basically gambling.

These myths spread because they sound confident and simple.

One common myth is that more activity equals better results. In soccer, running nonstop without purpose usually hurts the team. Financially, constantly trading, switching strategies, or chasing trends often does the same thing.

Another myth is that confidence equals competence. Athletes are competitive by nature. That confidence can turn into overconfidence with money. Just because you are comfortable taking risks on the field does not mean every financial risk is appropriate.

A third myth is that patience is passive. Players are taught to be aggressive, but smart aggression is controlled. Financial patience is not doing nothing. It is sticking to a plan even when emotions try to hijack it.

Locker room advice often ignores context. Who gave the advice. What their situation was. How much risk they could absorb. Without context, advice becomes noise.

Saving vs Investing vs Gambling

This confusion sits at the heart of most money mistakes.

Saving, investing, and gambling are not the same thing, but they often get lumped together.

Saving is about protection. It is the emergency fund. The money that keeps you from panicking when something unexpected happens. In soccer terms, saving is defensive shape. It does not win matches on its own, but without it, everything falls apart.

Investing is about long-term growth. It is planned. It is diversified. It accepts that there will be ups and downs, just like a season. Investing is the buildup play. It is not flashy, but it creates opportunities over time.

Gambling is chasing outcomes without a system. It is forcing shots from bad angles. It relies on luck more than preparation. Sometimes it works. Often it does not. The problem is that one lucky moment convinces people they have found a shortcut.

Athletes often confuse investing with gambling because both involve uncertainty. The difference is intent and structure. Investing follows a game plan. Gambling ignores one.

Why Patience Beats Panic

Soccer punishes panic quickly.

A rushed clearance invites pressure back. A forced pass creates a turnover. A player who abandons their position exposes the entire team.

Money works the same way.

Market drops, unexpected expenses, or bad headlines create emotional pressure. Panic tells you to do something now. Sell. Switch. Quit. Chase something else.

Patience tells you to zoom out.

Patience does not mean ignoring reality. It means responding, not reacting. It means understanding that seasons include bad stretches. That form changes. That fundamentals remain.

Most financial damage is not caused by bad plans. It is caused by abandoning good plans at the worst possible time.

Athletes understand this instinctively on the field. You do not scrap the system after one bad half. You make adjustments. You stay composed. You trust the work you put in.

The same mindset builds financial stability.

Coach's Perspective: What Would Your Coach Say?

Your coach would not tolerate chaos.

They would say things like:

Control what you can control.

Value the ball.

Trust the process.

Do not beat yourself.

One play at a time.

Financially, that translates into simple rules. Spend less than you earn. Build a base before chasing growth. Stick to a plan. Do not let emotion dictate decisions.

Coaches know that consistency beats intensity. Money rewards the same behavior.

Game Situations and Decision Points

Situation one. You hear about a hot investment everyone is talking about. Do you force the play, or do you stick to your system?

Situation two. The market drops and fear sets in. Do you panic and abandon your shape, or do you trust your positioning?

Situation three. You receive a sudden influx of money. Do you sprint forward and overcommit, or do you build possession first?

Each decision mirrors a moment on the pitch. The right answer usually feels boring in the moment and smart later.

Common Athlete Mistakes and Financial Parallels

Athletes rush because they are used to urgency. Money rewards patience.

Athletes chase highlights. Money rewards fundamentals.

Athletes trust confidence. Money requires verification.

Athletes hate sitting still. Money grows when left alone long enough.

Recognizing these patterns is the first step to breaking them.

Winning the Long Game

Soccer careers are short. Financial lives are long.

You do not win a season in one match. You do not build wealth in one decision. Success comes from stacking good days, good reps, and good habits.

This book is not about avoiding mistakes entirely. It is about building a system where mistakes do not define you.

Money feels confusing after soccer because no one taught you how to see the field. That changes now.

Athlete Takeaways

- Control possession before trying to score. Build savings before chasing growth.
- Do not confuse activity with progress. Smart teams move with purpose.
- Investing is buildup play. Gambling is forcing shots.
- Panic loses matches. Patience wins seasons.

Chapter 2: See the Whole Pitch: Your Financial Snapshot

Every good midfielder learns this lesson early.

If all you do is stare at the ball, you miss the game.

Great players scan constantly. Before the ball arrives, they check their shoulders. They see teammates, opponents, space, and danger. When the ball finally reaches them, the decision is already made because they understand the full picture.

Players who never look up panic. They get pressed. They lose possession. They feel rushed even when they are not.

Money works the same way.

If you only look at your bank balance, you are playing with your head down. You might survive for a while, but you are reacting instead of controlling the match.

A financial snapshot is learning to see the whole pitch.

Income, Expenses, and Cash Flow

Most people think income is the game. It is not.

Income is just one player on the field.

Cash flow is how the match actually feels. It is the movement of money in and out over time. You can earn a decent income and still feel broke if your expenses are sprinting ahead of you.

Athletes often experience this when their structure disappears. In-season routines vanish. Meals are no longer provided. Travel stipends stop. Small expenses stack up quietly.

Cash flow answers a simple question. After everything comes in and everything goes out, what actually happens?

Positive cash flow means you are keeping possession. Negative cash flow means you are constantly chasing.

The goal is not perfection. The goal is awareness. Until you see your cash flow clearly, you cannot improve it.

Assets, Liabilities, and Net Worth

Think of assets and liabilities like your squad depth.

Assets are things that can help you over time. Cash. Investments. Retirement accounts. Property. They either produce value or have the potential to.

Liabilities are obligations. Credit cards. Loans. Payments that pull resources away from future options.

Net worth is the scoreboard. Assets minus liabilities.

Many athletes avoid this number because it feels uncomfortable. That is understandable. But ignoring the scoreboard does not change the result.

In soccer, you do not pretend the score is different than it is. You adjust your strategy based on reality. Financially, net worth gives you that same clarity.

This is not about comparison. It is about context. Your number is your number. It is simply information.

Fixed vs Variable Expenses

Every team has fixed elements.

The pitch size does not change. The match length does not change. Certain roles are non-negotiable.

Financially, fixed expenses are the same way. Rent. Insurance. Minimum payments. These costs show up whether you feel like paying them or not.

Variable expenses are where decisions happen. Food. Travel. Entertainment. Subscriptions. Lifestyle choices.

Athletes often struggle here because variable expenses feel invisible. One coffee does not matter. One meal out does not matter. But seasons are not won on one play. They are won on patterns.

Understanding fixed versus variable expenses shows you where you actually have control. You do not need to eliminate fun. You need to know where flexibility exists.

Film Study on Where Your Money Actually Goes

This is the most important part of the chapter.

Film does not lie.

When coaches roll tape, excuses disappear. Effort. Positioning. Decision-making. It is all there.

Money film study works the same way.

Pull your statements. Look at the last three to six months. Categorize spending honestly. Not emotionally.

You will see surprises. Almost everyone does.

This is not about shame. It is about information. You cannot coach what you refuse to watch.

Most athletes discover they are not reckless. They are simply unaware. Small habits add up quietly until they become problems.

Once you see the film, adjustments become obvious.

Coach's Perspective: What Would Your Coach Say?

Your coach would not accept guessing.

They would say:

Know your role.

Do your job.

Details matter.

The film does not lie.

Control what you can control.

Financially, that means knowing your numbers. Not perfectly. Honestly.

You cannot manage what you refuse to measure. Great teams prepare because they understand reality.

Game Situations and Decision Points

Situation one. You get paid and feel comfortable. Do you spend freely because the balance looks good, or do you check the full picture?

Situation two. Expenses creep up and stress rises. Do you blame income, or do you review cash flow honestly?

Situation three. You consider a big purchase. Do you look at one month, or do you scan the whole season?

Each decision mirrors scanning the pitch before receiving the ball.

Common Athlete Mistakes and Financial Parallels

Athletes focus on income like goals scored. Money requires looking at assists, positioning, and buildup.

Athletes avoid film when it is uncomfortable. Money demands honesty before improvement.

Athletes chase feelings. Money rewards clarity.

Athletes assume effort alone fixes problems. Money requires structure.

Winning the Long Game

You cannot control a match you cannot see.

Seeing the whole pitch does not mean everything changes overnight. It means decisions improve immediately.

Financial snapshots are not one-time events. They are regular check-ins. Just like film sessions, they keep small issues from becoming big ones.

When you know your numbers, panic fades. Confidence grows. Possession improves.

This chapter is not about restriction. It is about control.

Athlete Takeaways

- Lift your head. Know where your money is coming from and where it is going.
- Cash flow tells you how the match is actually playing out.
- Assets build options. Liabilities limit them.
- Watch the film. The truth creates better decisions.

Chapter 3: Building Possession: Budgeting and Saving

In soccer, possession is not about flair. It is about control.

Teams that dominate possession are not always the fastest or flashiest. They are disciplined. They know where the next pass is coming from. They move with intention. They protect the ball because they understand what possession gives them: time, options, and composure.

Budgeting and saving work the same way.

When you control your money, you control tempo. When you do not, the game speeds up, decisions get rushed, and mistakes multiply. This chapter is about building possession with your finances so you are not constantly reacting to pressure.

Budgeting Systems That Actually Work

Most athletes hate the word budget because it sounds restrictive.

They picture spreadsheets, rules, and someone telling them what they cannot do. That mindset misses the point. A budget is not a cage. It is a system.

In soccer terms, a budget is your shape. It gives structure so you can play freely inside it.

Good budgets are simple. They focus on flow, not perfection. You do not need to track every penny forever. You need a clear understanding of where money comes in, where it goes out, and what remains available.

There are a few systems that actually work for athletes:

One is the percentage system. Income gets divided into buckets. Living expenses, saving, investing, and lifestyle. This works well when income fluctuates because percentages adjust automatically.

Another is the fixed-first system. You decide savings and investing first, then live on what remains. This mirrors training. You schedule practice first, then fit life around it.

The key is consistency. A perfect budget used once is useless. A simple budget followed every month builds control.

Budgeting fails when it becomes emotional. It succeeds when it becomes routine.

Automating Savings Like Daily Training

No athlete relies on motivation alone.

You train because it is scheduled. You lift because it is programmed. You recover because it is part of the plan. Saving works best the same way.

Automation removes decision-making. Money moves before you can overthink it. That is not weakness. That is discipline.

Automated savings are like daily training sessions. Small, repeated actions compound into results. One lift does not make you strong. One save does not change your future. Hundreds of reps do.

When savings are automatic, you stop negotiating with yourself. You stop asking if this month is different. You trust the system.

Athletes often wait until the end of the month to save. That is like training only if you feel good. It rarely works.

Pay yourself first. Automate it. Let the reps stack quietly.

Emergency Funds as Injury Protection

Every athlete understands injury risk.

You do not expect to get hurt, but you prepare for it anyway. You train properly. You warm up. You carry insurance. You respect recovery.

An emergency fund is financial injury protection.

It is not about return. It is about resilience.

Unexpected expenses happen. Jobs change. Income pauses. Life does not care about your timing. Without an emergency fund, every surprise becomes a crisis.

With one, surprises become inconveniences.

The goal is not luxury. The goal is breathing room. Enough cash to handle problems without selling investments, taking on debt, or panicking.

This is possession in its purest form. When something goes wrong, you keep the ball instead of clearing it blindly.

Balancing Lifestyle With Long-Term Goals

Athletes are wired to enjoy life now.

You have trained hard. You have sacrificed. You want to live. That is normal.

The mistake is thinking enjoyment and discipline are opposites. They are not.

Great teams manage energy across the season. They do not sprint nonstop. They choose moments to push and moments to recover.

Financially, balance works the same way.

You do not need to eliminate lifestyle spending. You need to decide what actually matters. Spend intentionally. Cut mindless spending. Keep the things that add real value to your life.

Lifestyle inflation is what happens when spending grows without thought. It sneaks in quietly. Subscriptions. Upgrades. Convenience purchases. None feel dangerous alone. Together, they drain possession.

Long-term goals require space. Saving and investing are how you create that space.

Balance is not about restriction. It is about alignment. Your money should support the life you want, not compete with it.

Coach's Perspective: What Would Your Coach Say?

Your coach would not let the team play without structure.

They would say:

Value the ball.

Trust the system.

Reps matter.

Details win games.

Do your job.

Financially, that means showing up consistently. Saving when it feels boring. Sticking to the plan when distractions appear. Not abandoning structure for short-term comfort.

Coaches know something athletes forget after sports. Freedom comes from discipline.

Game Situations and Decision Points

Situation one. You get a raise or bonus. Do you immediately upgrade your lifestyle, or do you increase savings first?

Situation two. An unexpected expense hits. Do you use an emergency fund calmly, or do you reach for debt in a panic?

Situation three. Friends are spending freely. Do you follow the crowd, or do you stick to your own game plan?

Each decision tests possession. The right choice rarely feels exciting in the moment. It feels obvious later.

Common Athlete Mistakes and Financial Parallels

Athletes confuse intensity with progress. Money rewards consistency.

Athletes skip fundamentals because they are boring. Money collapses without them.

Athletes rely on motivation. Money requires systems.

Athletes chase lifestyle rewards too early. Money punishes impatience.

Recognizing these patterns helps you avoid repeating them.

Winning the Long Game

Possession does not win every match immediately. It wins seasons.

Budgeting and saving are not about saying no to life. They are about saying yes to your future with confidence.

When you control your money, stress drops. Decisions slow down. Opportunities open up. You stop reacting and start dictating tempo.

That is the real goal. Not perfection. Control.

Athlete Takeaways

- Possession creates options. Budgeting creates control.
- Automate savings like training reps. Consistency beats motivation.
- Emergency funds protect you when life hits unexpectedly.
- Balance lifestyle and long-term goals by spending with intention.

Chapter 4: Playing With Borrowed Time: Credit and Debt

Credit and debt are like playing on a clock that is not yours. You get access to resources now, but there is always a timer running in the background. Interest is ticking. Payments are coming. Deadlines do not care how you feel that month. Decisions today shape how much freedom you have tomorrow.

In sports, you can feel the game clock. You see it. You adjust strategy based on it. In money, the clock is quieter. You do not hear interest accumulating. You do not see stress building in real time. But it is happening.

Used correctly, credit can help you move forward. It can open doors, smooth out timing, and allow you to make strategic moves. Used poorly, it drains momentum, limits options, and forces you into defensive decisions for years.

This chapter is about understanding how the clock works so you are not surprised when time runs out.

How Credit Scores and Reports Work

Think of your credit report as game film and your credit score as the coach's evaluation of that film.

The report shows what you have actually done. Accounts opened. Payments made. Balances carried. Limits used. Mistakes included. Nothing is based on your intentions. It is based on your patterns.

The score summarizes how risky you look based on that history. Lenders are not asking if you are a good person. They are asking, "Based on the film, how likely is this player to make the right play consistently?"

Credit scores are built around a few core factors.

Payment history matters most.

Paying on time consistently shows discipline. Missing payments shows breakdowns in fundamentals. One missed payment can stay on your report for years, just like a costly turnover in a championship game gets remembered.

Balances matter.

High balances relative to your limits signal poor possession. Even if you pay on time, carrying too much debt makes you look unstable. You are using too much of the field and leaving no room to maneuver.

Length of history matters.

Longevity builds trust. A long track record of responsible behavior tells lenders you are predictable in a good way. This is why opening and closing accounts constantly can hurt. You are erasing film that shows you can be consistent.

New credit matters.

Too many new accounts at once looks like panic or overextension. It can signal that you are scrambling for resources instead of following a plan.

Mix matters.

A variety of credit types, like credit cards, installment loans, and other accounts, shows you can handle different responsibilities. It is like being a well rounded athlete who can play multiple roles.

None of this is personal. It is pattern recognition. Credit systems reward consistency and punish chaos.

Credit Cards, Loans, and Interest

Credit cards are the fastest way to lose control if you do not understand them.

They feel harmless because minimum payments are small. You swipe, and nothing dramatic happens. But interest compounds quietly. Carrying balances month after month turns convenience into a tax on your future.

A balance that seems manageable can double over time if you only make minimum payments. That is not because you are lazy. It is because the system is designed to stretch repayment out and maximize interest.

Loans work the same way, just slower. Auto loans, student loans, personal loans, mortgages. Each one comes with a cost for borrowing time. You get the benefit now. You commit future income to repay it.

Interest is the opponent you never see. It does not trash talk. It does not show emotion. It just keeps scoring.

Athletes often underestimate interest because they think in short bursts. One month does not feel expensive. One year barely registers. Ten years changes everything. Small rates over long periods become big numbers.

Borrowing money means committing future effort before you earn it. That is not always bad, but it must be intentional.

Good Debt vs Bad Debt

Not all debt is equal.

Good debt is usually tied to long term benefit and manageable risk. Education that increases earning potential. Housing that fits your budget and needs. Business investments with clear plans and realistic expectations.

Bad debt is usually tied to consumption. Lifestyle upgrades. Impulse purchases. Status spending. Things that fade while the payments remain.

The difference is not moral. It is strategic.

Good debt supports progress. It helps you build skills, stability, or opportunity. Bad debt steals future flexibility. It locks you into payments that limit your choices.

The key question is simple. Does this debt make tomorrow easier or harder?

If the answer is harder, think twice. If it reduces future freedom, you are trading long term control for short term comfort.

Debt Traps That Kill Momentum

Debt traps rarely appear as disasters at first. They build slowly and quietly.

One trap is **minimum payment thinking**. Paying only the minimum feels responsible because you are technically on time. But you are barely touching the principal. You are running on a treadmill, not moving down the field.

Another trap is **lifestyle inflation funded by credit**. Income goes up. Spending follows. Debt fills the gap when discipline disappears. Instead of using higher income to build stability, you use it to support higher payments.

Another is **emotional borrowing**. Stress purchases. Comfort spending. Using credit to cope rather than plan. After a tough week, a purchase feels like relief. The bill later feels like pressure.

Athletes fall into these traps because they are used to pushing through discomfort. In training, effort solves problems. With debt, effort alone does not fix the math. Interest does not care how hard you work.

Once momentum slows, options shrink. Stress increases. Decisions become reactive instead of strategic. Debt turns small mistakes into long term consequences.

Coach's Perspective: What Would Your Coach Say?

Your coach would not let you play recklessly.

They would say:

Value the ball.

Know the clock.

Do not put the team in a bad position.

Make the simple play.

Finish strong.

Financially, that means borrowing with purpose, not emotion. Paying on time, every time. Reducing balances, not just maintaining them. Avoiding unnecessary risks just because you feel confident.

Coaches understand that discipline protects the team. Debt discipline protects your future self.

Game Situations and Decision Points

Situation one. You want something now but do not have the cash.

Do you wait and save, or do you borrow and pay later? Waiting builds discipline and keeps the clock on your side. Borrowing speeds things up but starts the timer.

Situation two. You carry balances but keep spending.

Do you slow down and regain possession, or do you hope it works itself out? Hope is not a strategy in sports or money.

Situation three. You qualify for more credit.

Do you use it because you can, or because it fits the plan? Just because the coach says you can take the shot does not mean it is the right one.

Each choice either preserves momentum or bleeds it away.

Common Athlete Mistakes and Financial Parallels

Athletes play through pain. Debt pain compounds quietly.

Athletes trust confidence. Credit systems reward consistency, not bravado.

Athletes chase upgrades early. Debt punishes impatience.

Athletes underestimate recovery time. Debt recovery takes longer than expected.

Understanding these parallels keeps you from repeating them.

Winning the Long Game

Debt is not evil. It is powerful.

Power without control is dangerous.

The goal is not to avoid borrowing forever. The goal is to borrow intentionally and repay aggressively. Keep the clock working for you, not against you.

When debt shrinks, options expand. Stress drops. Flexibility increases.

Momentum returns. You stop playing defense all the time and start choosing your plays again.

That is how you stop playing on borrowed time and start controlling the match.

Athlete Takeaways

Credit is a clock. Know how much time you are borrowing.

Interest scores quietly against you if you lose discipline.

Good debt builds future options. Bad debt steals them.

Momentum dies when debt replaces planning.

Consistency, not confidence, wins the long game.

Chapter 5: The Clubhouse of Money: Banking Basics

Banking is not exciting, but it is foundational.

No one puts "opened a great checking account" on a highlight reel. There are no celebrations for setting up automatic transfers. No trophies for reading fee schedules. But just like stretching, film study, and recovery work, the boring fundamentals are what keep everything else from falling apart.

Every team needs a clubhouse. It is where gear is stored, meetings happen, and routines are built. It is not glamorous, but it is essential. When the clubhouse is organized, the team moves with rhythm. Players know where their equipment is. Trainers know where supplies are. Coaches can focus on strategy instead of chaos.

When the clubhouse is a mess, everything feels harder than it should. You waste time. You forget things. Stress builds before you even step onto the field.

Your bank accounts serve the same role. They are the base of operations for your financial life. Paychecks land there. Bills leave from there. Savings are staged there. Investments are funded from there. If this foundation is sloppy, even smart financial decisions downstream become stressful.

This chapter is about understanding how the clubhouse works so you can move through it with confidence instead of confusion.

Checking vs Savings Accounts

Think in terms of roles on a team.

Checking accounts are for movement.

They handle day to day transactions. Income comes in. Expenses go out. Bills get paid. Debit cards, online payments, transfers. This is where money flows in real time. It is active, like a player constantly involved in the play.

Savings accounts are for separation.

They hold money you do not want mixed with daily spending. Emergency funds. Short term goals. Planned expenses like travel, equipment, or off season costs. Savings creates distance between money you use and money you protect. It plays defense.

The biggest mistake athletes make is using one account for everything. That is like throwing practice gear, game uniforms, recovery tools, and medical equipment into one pile on the clubhouse floor. Eventually, something important goes missing. You do not know what is available and what is already spoken for.

When rent, food, subscriptions, and random spending all mix with your emergency fund, your brain starts lying to you. You see a big number and assume you are safe. Then real life hits, and suddenly you are short.

Checking is active. Savings is defensive.

Offense scores. Defense protects the lead.

When the two are clearly separated, control improves immediately. You stop guessing. You start knowing.

Online Banks vs Traditional Banks

Choosing a bank is like choosing a training environment.

Traditional banks offer physical branches, face to face service, and familiarity. For some people, that access matters a lot. Especially when dealing with complicated issues, large transactions, or emotional situations. Walking into a branch and talking to a person can bring clarity and reassurance.

Online banks often offer higher interest rates on savings, lower fees, and strong digital tools. They operate efficiently because they do not carry the cost of physical locations. That efficiency often gets passed on to customers in the form of better terms.

Neither is automatically better. The right choice depends on how you operate.

Some athletes value in person access. Others are fully comfortable managing everything through apps and websites. Many use a hybrid approach. Checking at a traditional bank for accessibility and convenience. Savings at an online bank to earn more and avoid fees.

The key is understanding what you are paying for.

Fees reduce possession. Interest earned builds it.

Just like in sports, you do not pick a facility because it looks good. You pick it because it helps you perform.

How Money Moves Globally

Soccer is global. Basketball is global. Track, tennis, dance, and many other sports are global too. Money is just as global.

Athletes often travel, study abroad, compete internationally, or work with teams and organizations in different countries. Understanding how money moves across borders matters more than people realize.

Currency exchange rates change constantly. What looks like a small difference can become meaningful over large amounts. Transfer fees hide in the background. Timing affects outcomes.

International wires, payment apps, and digital platforms all move money differently. Some are fast and expensive. Others are slower but cheaper. Some offer better exchange rates. Others build profit into the rate you receive.

The mistake is assuming money moves instantly and freely everywhere. It does not.

Planning ahead avoids surprises. Knowing the costs avoids frustration. Awareness helps you keep more of what you earn.

Possession matters in sports. It matters with money too.

Protecting Yourself From Fraud and Overdrafts

Fraud is pressure from an unseen opponent.

Scammers do not win by strength. They win by distraction. They exploit speed, fear, and urgency. They rely on emotional reactions, not logic. Athletes are often targets because they are public, busy, and sometimes inexperienced with large sums of money.

Strong passwords, two factor authentication, and account alerts are not paranoia. They are fundamentals. They are like wearing proper gear and following safety protocols. You hope nothing happens, but you prepare anyway.

Overdrafts are a different type of breakdown. They happen when timing is off. A bill clears before income hits. A forgotten subscription renews. A small miscalculation turns into multiple fees.

The solution is not perfection. It is systems.

Keep a buffer in checking.

Turn on balance alerts.

Review accounts regularly.

Defense matters even when nothing seems wrong. Championship teams respect defense even when they are winning.

Coach's Perspective: What Would Your Coach Say?

Your coach would demand organization.

They would say:

Handle your business.

Protect the locker room.

Details matter.

Do not beat yourself.

Be prepared.

Financially, that means clean accounts, clear roles, and systems that prevent avoidable mistakes.

Good teams lose games because of turnovers, penalties, and mental errors. Not lack of talent. Financially, the same thing happens. People struggle not because they cannot earn, but because systems are sloppy.

Eliminate self inflicted errors, and your performance improves fast.

Game Situations and Decision Points

Situation one. You keep dipping into savings for daily spending.

Do you fix the structure, or keep reacting? This is not a willpower issue. It is a system issue. Adjust transfers. Rebuild boundaries.

Situation two. You see a new bank offering better terms.

Do you evaluate thoughtfully, or stick with comfort without review? Loyalty is great in sports. In banking, you still need to check if your setup is helping or hurting you.

Situation three. You receive a suspicious message asking for account details.

Do you react quickly, or pause and verify? One calm decision can prevent months of stress.

Each moment tests discipline, not intelligence.

Common Athlete Mistakes and Financial Parallels

Athletes overlook basics when things feel fine. Money breaks when fundamentals are ignored.

Athletes rely on familiarity. Money rewards evaluation.

Athletes assume speed equals efficiency. Money punishes rushed decisions.

Athletes focus on offense. Money requires defense at all times.

The fundamentals are boring until they save you.

Winning the Long Game

Banking is not where wealth is built, but it is where mistakes are prevented.

When your clubhouse is organized, everything else flows. Payments happen smoothly. Savings grow quietly. Opportunities are easier to act on. Stress drops.

You stop worrying about logistics and start focusing on bigger decisions like investing, career moves, business ideas, and life goals.

That is the advantage of strong fundamentals. You create stability, and stability creates freedom.

Athlete Takeaways

Separate checking and savings to protect possession.

Choose banks based on function, not habit.

Understand how money moves before you need it.

Defense matters. Protect accounts and avoid unnecessary fees.

Strong systems reduce stress and prevent self inflicted losses.

Banking is not flashy, but championships are built on fundamentals.

Part II: Defensive Shape and Protection

Clean sheets come from discipline and positioning.

In soccer, the best defenses are rarely dramatic. They are organized, disciplined, and positioned correctly before danger develops. Players communicate, stay compact, and trust the system. Because of that, problems are handled early and quietly.

Financial protection works the same way.

Most financial setbacks are not caused by one huge mistake. They come from small gaps. Missing coverage. Ignored risks. Assuming nothing will go wrong because nothing has gone wrong yet.

Defensive shape in your finances means preparing for uncertainty without panic. Health issues, accidents, income disruptions, and legal risks are part of life. Protection exists to make sure one unexpected event does not undo years of progress.

Insurance, cash reserves, and basic planning are your back line. They do not create growth, but they keep you in the match when something goes wrong.

Discipline matters. Protection breaks down when people get careless, let coverage lapse, or fail to review what they actually have. Positioning matters too. Too little coverage leaves you exposed. Too much wastes resources.

Clean sheets are built through habits, not heroics.

When your financial defense is solid, you play with confidence. You make smarter decisions. You take calculated risks without fear of one mistake ending the season.

Chapter 6: Risk Awareness and Decision Making

Risk is always present. The difference between smart players and reckless ones is not fearlessness. It is awareness.

In soccer, risk shows up in every decision. When to step. When to hold. When to press high. When to drop into shape. When to switch the field. When to clear your lines instead of forcing a pass.

Teams that misread risk get exposed. A bad step leads to an open lane. One player pressing alone leaves space behind. A careless pass turns into a counterattack. Suddenly the game changes.

Teams that understand risk control tempo. They bend without breaking. They survive pressure. They know when to attack and when to stabilize.

Money works the same way. Risk is not something you avoid completely. It is something you manage with intention.

Emotional Risk vs Financial Risk

Athletes are comfortable with emotional risk.

You are used to pressure. Crowds. Expectations. Big moments. You have taken shots with the game on the line. You have performed in environments where one mistake feels massive. Emotionally, you trust yourself to respond. That confidence is earned.

Financial risk is different.

Emotional risk is how uncertainty feels. Financial risk is how much damage you can actually absorb.

A decision can feel exciting and still be dangerous. Another can feel boring and be incredibly powerful. Confusing those two is where many athletes get into trouble.

You might feel calm investing in something volatile because you are used to high pressure. But if a downturn would force you into debt, derail your education, delay rent, or make you sell at the worst time, the risk is too high, no matter how confident you feel.

Your emotional strength does not automatically increase your financial capacity.

Smart decisions separate emotion from exposure. The question is not "Can I handle the stress?" The question is "Can my situation handle the loss?"

Time Horizon and Flexibility

Time changes everything.

A short time horizon requires caution. A long one allows patience.

In soccer, you play differently in the 5th minute than the 85th. Scoreline matters. Fatigue matters. Substitutions matter. Context shapes decisions. If you are protecting a lead late, you do not take the same risks you would early in the match.

Financially, time horizon is your context.

Money needed soon should not be treated the same as money meant for years down the road. Rent next month is not the same as retirement decades away. Tuition due next semester is not the same as long term investments.

The closer the deadline, the less room you have for volatility. If the money must be there on a specific date, you cannot afford large swings.

Flexibility also matters. If you have savings, low fixed expenses, and multiple income options, you can take more risk. If your budget is tight and one setback would cause problems, your risk capacity is lower.

Athletes often make mistakes by treating all money the same. Emergency funds, travel money, daily expenses, and long term investments all serve different roles. Mixing them increases risk without realizing it.

Risk tolerance increases with time and flexibility. It decreases when deadlines and obligations get closer.

How Risk Affects Every Decision

Risk is not just about investing.

It shows up in spending, saving, career moves, borrowing, and lifestyle choices.

Taking on a big fixed expense like a high rent, expensive car, or large loan increases risk because it reduces flexibility. Now more of your income is locked in before you even make choices.

Carrying high debt magnifies mistakes. One missed paycheck or unexpected expense has a bigger impact. Ignoring insurance or emergency savings exposes you to setbacks that have nothing to do with markets at all.

Choosing not to build skills or plan for life after sport is also a risk. It limits future options and increases pressure later.

Every decision either increases or decreases your margin for error.

The goal is not to eliminate risk. That is impossible. The goal is to make sure one decision does not put the entire match at risk.

Knowing When to Press and When to Drop

Pressing can win games. It can also leave you exposed.

Good teams press with purpose. They read body language. They recognize when the opponent is off balance. They make sure support is behind them. They press together.

Dropping into shape is not weakness. It is discipline. It protects against unnecessary damage and keeps the game in front of you.

Financially, pressing looks like taking calculated risks when you have time, savings, stable income, and a plan. Starting a business, investing for growth, pursuing opportunities. You are moving forward with structure behind you.

Dropping looks like protecting capital when uncertainty rises or flexibility shrinks. Building cash reserves. Reducing debt. Avoiding big commitments during unstable periods. Stabilizing before attacking again.

Problems happen when people press out of emotion instead of strategy. Chasing returns because others are. Making big moves out of fear of missing out. Acting fast because the crowd is loud.

Risk aware players read the situation first. Then they move.

Coach's Perspective: What Would Your Coach Say?

Your coach would not want reckless aggression.

They would say:

Control what you can control.

Stay composed.

Play smart.

Know the situation.

Trust your positioning.

Financially, that means understanding your exposure before acting. Knowing your timeline. Respecting your limits. Playing within your system instead of someone else's.

Coaches know that discipline under pressure separates winners from costly mistakes.

Game Situations and Decision Points

Situation one. Markets are volatile and emotions are high.

Do you react to noise or stick to your plan? Volatility feels like chaos, but reacting emotionally often increases risk instead of reducing it.

Situation two. A high risk opportunity appears.

Do you evaluate fit, timing, and downside, or chase excitement? Just because something has big upside does not mean it fits your situation.

Situation three. Life changes reduce flexibility. Injury. Job change. Family responsibilities.

Do you adjust risk accordingly or pretend nothing changed? Refusing to adapt increases exposure quietly.

Each decision mirrors reading the field under pressure. The best players slow the moment down instead of speeding it up.

Common Athlete Mistakes and Financial Parallels

Athletes confuse courage with recklessness. Money punishes that mistake.

Athletes trust confidence over context. Money demands context.

Athletes press alone. Money requires support, structure, and backup plans.

Athletes ignore fatigue. Financial strain compounds quietly until performance drops.

Recognizing these patterns helps you stay composed instead of reactive.

Winning the Long Game

Risk awareness is not about playing scared. It is about playing smart.

The best teams manage risk across the entire season, not just one game. They accept that not every moment is for attack. They protect leads. They rotate players. They conserve energy. They finish strong.

Financial success works the same way.

When you understand risk, decisions slow down. Panic fades. Confidence becomes grounded in reality. You stop forcing plays and start controlling matches.

You accept that stability is not boring. It is strategic.

Athlete Takeaways

Emotional confidence does not equal financial capacity.

Time horizon and flexibility determine how much risk you can take.

Every decision changes your margin for error.

Press with support. Drop with discipline.

Smart players read the situation before they move.

Chapter 7: Insurance Fundamentals Every Player Needs

Insurance is not exciting, but it is essential.

In soccer, defense is not about hero tackles or dramatic slides. It is about positioning, communication, awareness, and making sure one mistake does not turn into a goal. The best defenses often go unnoticed because nothing bad happens.

Insurance plays the same role in your financial life. It does not help you score. It does not grow your money. It does not feel productive in the moment. But it keeps you from getting knocked out of the match by something you never saw coming.

Most athletes do not think about insurance until they are forced to. An injury. A car accident. A medical bill. A lawsuit. By then, options are limited and decisions are rushed. That is when stress replaces strategy.

This chapter is about understanding the basics so protection is intentional, not reactive.

Health Insurance Basics

Health insurance is the most important coverage most players will ever carry.

In structured environments like school, national programs, or professional teams, coverage often exists automatically. Someone else handles enrollment. Someone else pays most of the cost. It feels normal.

Once that structure disappears, responsibility shifts to you. This is where many athletes get caught off guard. A gap in coverage of even a few months can become extremely expensive if something happens.

Health insurance protects you from catastrophic costs. One injury, illness, or emergency room visit can create bills that take years to recover from if you are uninsured or underinsured. It is not just about doctor visits. It is about financial survival.

Key concepts matter.

Networks determine where you can receive care at the best cost. Going outside the network often means paying much more.

Deductibles determine how much you pay out of pocket before coverage really kicks in. A low premium plan with a very high deductible means you carry more of the early cost.

Out-of-pocket maximums define the worst case scenario in a bad year. This is one of the most important numbers on your plan. It tells you the cap on what you might have to pay yourself.

The goal is not perfect coverage. That would be too expensive for most people. The goal is survivable risk. You want to know that a health issue does not become a financial crisis.

Auto and Renters Insurance

Auto insurance is mandatory in most places, but minimum coverage is rarely enough.

There are different parts to auto coverage.

Liability coverage protects you if you cause injury or damage to other people. This is critical. If you cause a serious accident and your limits are low, your future income and assets can be at risk.

Property coverage protects your own vehicle. Whether this makes sense depends on the value of the car and your ability to replace it.

Many athletes focus on keeping the monthly premium low. But one accident can follow you for years if limits are too low. That is not worth a small monthly savings.

Renters insurance is often overlooked and almost always inexpensive.

It protects your belongings like clothes, electronics, and equipment. But the real value is **liability protection**. If someone gets hurt in your apartment, or you accidentally cause damage to someone else's property, renters insurance can protect you from lawsuits and large claims.

Many athletes skip renters insurance because they think they do not own enough to justify it. They think about couches and TVs. The real protection is against legal and liability risk, not just stuff.

Homeowners Insurance

Homeowners insurance is a bigger version of renters insurance with added complexity.

It protects the structure of the home, your belongings, and your liability. But it also introduces risks people do not understand until after a loss.

Home values change. Construction costs rise. If coverage limits are too low, you may not have enough to rebuild after major damage. That is called underinsurance, and it is more common than people realize.

Policies also contain exclusions. Certain types of damage may not be covered unless you add specific endorsements. Floods, earthquakes, and other events often require separate policies.

Owning a home without adequate insurance is like playing with an exposed back line. Everything feels fine until one play breaks through.

Policies should be reviewed periodically, not just when you buy the house.

Deductibles, Premiums, and Coverage Limits

These three terms define how insurance actually works.

Premiums are what you pay to keep coverage active. Think of it as your defensive training cost. You pay consistently to stay protected.

Deductibles are what you pay out of pocket before coverage applies. Higher deductibles usually mean lower premiums, but more risk on you if something happens.

Coverage limits define how much protection you actually have. This is the maximum the insurance company will pay.

Lower premiums often mean higher deductibles or lower limits. Higher limits mean stronger protection but higher cost.

There is no universal right answer. The correct balance depends on savings, income stability, and overall risk tolerance. If you have strong savings, you might handle a higher deductible. If cash flow is tight, a lower deductible might make more sense.

Athletes often focus only on monthly cost. That is a mistake. The real question is what happens when something goes wrong.

Coach's Perspective: What Would Your Coach Say?

Your coach would not ignore defense.

They would say:

Protect the team.

Do not leave gaps.

Details matter.

Be prepared.

Handle your business.

Financially, that means knowing what you are covered for and what you are not. Reviewing policies. Asking questions. Not assuming that because you have a policy, everything is handled.

Good defense is quiet and boring. That is the point. When insurance is working properly, you rarely think about it.

Game Situations and Decision Points

Situation one. You choose the cheapest insurance option.

Do you understand what you gave up in limits or coverage? Cheap can be expensive later.

Situation two. Life changes. New job. New home. New car. New city.

Do you update coverage or assume it still fits? Insurance that was right last year might be wrong now.

Situation three. A claim happens.

Are you prepared, or are you learning the rules in the moment? Stress is not the time to first read your policy.

Each decision affects how well you are protected when pressure hits.

Common Athlete Mistakes and Financial Parallels

Athletes underestimate risk until it appears. Insurance exists for what you cannot predict.

Athletes focus on performance and ignore protection. Money punishes that imbalance.

Athletes assume coverage is automatic. Outside structured environments, it is not.

Athletes delay boring decisions. Insurance failures are rarely convenient.

Strong systems are built before the crisis, not during it.

Winning the Long Game

Insurance does not make you rich. It keeps you solvent.

It protects progress. It preserves options. It keeps one bad moment from erasing years of work.

Strong defense allows confident offense. When you know a setback will not destroy you financially, you make better decisions everywhere else. You take smart risks. You plan longer term. You operate with less fear.

That is the role insurance plays in your financial life. Quiet protection that keeps you in the game.

Athlete Takeaways

Insurance is defense. It keeps one mistake from ending the season.

Health coverage is foundational. Gaps are expensive.

Liability protection often matters more than possessions.

Review coverage as life changes.

Balance premiums, deductibles, and limits with your real risk, not just your monthly budget.

Chapter 8: Life, Disability, and Liability Protection

Some risks announce themselves. Others sit quietly until the moment they change everything.

A missed bill announces itself. A tight budget announces itself. But death, disability, and major liability events often show up without warning. They are low frequency, high impact risks. You may go years with nothing happening, then one moment changes the trajectory of everything.

Life, disability, and liability protection are not about everyday inconveniences. They are about guarding against events that are unlikely, but severe. These are the moments that do not show up in your monthly spending but can wipe out years of discipline if ignored.

Athletes understand this concept instinctively. You train to prevent injury, not because you expect to get hurt today, but because you respect the possibility. You warm up even when you feel fine. You wear protection not because you are scared, but because you are serious.

Financial protection works the same way.

Term vs Permanent Life Insurance

Life insurance exists for one primary reason: to protect people who depend on your income.

If no one relies on your earnings, life insurance may be unnecessary or minimal right now. But if others depend on you, a spouse, children, parents, or business partners, coverage becomes part of your responsibility, not just an option.

Term life insurance is straightforward. Coverage lasts for a defined period, often aligned with working years, mortgage timelines, or the years children are financially dependent. It is typically affordable and designed to solve real problems. Replacing income. Paying off loans. Giving your family time to adjust if something happens to you.

It is clean protection. High coverage for a defined time at a relatively low cost.

Permanent life insurance lasts for your entire life and includes long-term financial features alongside the insurance. These policies can play a role in certain advanced planning situations, but they are more complex, more expensive, and frequently misunderstood.

Many players are sold permanent insurance before they understand the basics. Complexity too early creates confusion and misalignment. For most athletes, especially early and mid career, term insurance covers the core risk efficiently.

The key is alignment. Coverage should match responsibility. Nothing more. Nothing less. Insurance is not about collecting policies. It is about covering real exposure.

Disability Insurance and Income Protection

Your ability to earn income is your most valuable asset.

You can insure your car. You can insure your home. But your future earning power often dwarfs the value of anything you own. If that income stops, everything else gets stressed.

Disability insurance protects you if injury or illness prevents you from working. This risk is often underestimated because it does not feel dramatic like a single accident. But statistically, disability during working years is more common than early death.

Many athletes assume they are covered through employers, leagues, or government programs. That assumption is dangerous. Coverage may be limited, delayed, or capped far below what you need to maintain your lifestyle and responsibilities.

Details matter here.

How is disability defined? Can you not work in your specific profession, or any job?

How much income is replaced?

How long do benefits last?

How long must you wait before benefits begin?

Disability insurance is not about comfort. It is about continuity. It keeps rent paid, food on the table, and long-term plans intact when earning pauses unexpectedly.

Umbrella Liability Coverage

Liability risk grows as your visibility, assets, and income grow.

Umbrella insurance provides additional protection beyond your auto, renters, or homeowners policies. It steps in when basic coverage limits are exceeded.

Athletes are often more exposed than they realize. You may drive more. Travel more. Be more visible. Accidents, misunderstandings, and lawsuits do not always depend on intent. They depend on circumstances, and sometimes perception.

A serious accident or claim can exceed basic policy limits quickly. Without additional protection, personal assets and future income may be at risk.

Umbrella coverage is designed to protect your future, not just your present. It is often inexpensive relative to the protection it provides, which makes it one of the most efficient defensive tools available.

Ignoring liability risk is like leaving space behind the back line and hoping no one notices. Sooner or later, someone will.

Common Insurance Mistakes Players Make

One mistake is assuming coverage exists without verifying it. "I think I'm covered" is not a plan.

Another mistake is buying based on price alone. Cheap coverage that fails when needed is not savings. It is risk disguised as efficiency.

Some players rely entirely on advice without understanding the recommendation. Others delay decisions because they feel boring or uncomfortable compared to growth and opportunity topics.

Insurance mistakes rarely announce themselves early. They show up when options are limited, emotions are high, and decisions are urgent.

Coach's Perspective: What Would Your Coach Say?

Your coach would not ignore availability or protection.

They would say:

Protect your ability to play.

Do not put the team at risk.

Handle your responsibilities.

Prepare before it matters.

Details win games.

Financially, that means protecting income and dependents first, not after everything else is built. Offense is exciting. Defense keeps the season alive.

Game Situations and Decision Points

Situation one. You are offered a policy you do not fully understand.

Do you pause and learn, or do you sign because the presentation sounded confident?

Situation two. You assume work coverage is enough.

Have you read the details, or are you trusting a summary?

Situation three. Your life changes. Marriage. Kids. Business ownership.

Do you adjust protection or ignore the shift in responsibility?

Each decision affects how exposed you really are, not how protected you feel.

Common Athlete Mistakes and Financial Parallels

Athletes assume strength equals invincibility. Financial risk does not care how strong you are.

Athletes delay boring preparation. Insurance failures are rarely convenient.

Athletes trust systems without checking details. Money punishes assumptions.

Athletes focus on upside and forget protection. Long careers and stable lives require defense first.

Winning the Long Game

Life, disability, and liability protection do not create wealth. They protect it.

They keep progress intact. They preserve options. They prevent one moment from undoing years of disciplined decisions.

When protection is in place, confidence rises. Decisions improve. You play freer knowing the foundation is secure. You can focus on growth because you know one setback will not end the match.

That is the purpose of this chapter. Quiet defense that allows long term success.

Athlete Takeaways

Protect income before chasing growth. Availability matters.

Term life insurance often solves early and mid career needs cleanly.

Disability risk is real and commonly underestimated.

Liability protection defends what you are building for the long run.

Defense first. Offense second. That is how careers last.

Part III: Building the Attack (Investing Fundamentals)

G*oals come from buildup, not desperation shots.*

In soccer, goals rarely come from chaos. They come from patience, spacing, and trust in the system.

The buildup matters. Moving the ball through midfield. Creating angles. Waiting for the right moment instead of forcing a shot that is not there. Teams that rely on desperation rarely score consistently. Teams that build intelligently create chances over and over again.

Investing works the same way.

This section is not about chasing hot tips, timing the perfect moment, or trying to score with one big move. It is about building an attack that works across seasons, not just highlights.

Athletes often struggle with investing because the pace feels wrong. Progress feels slow. Results are not immediate. There is no scoreboard updating every rep. That discomfort leads many people to force plays, constantly change strategies, or abandon the plan when things get quiet or volatile.

Smart investing rewards patience.

Just like in soccer, the ball does not move forward on its own. It moves because of positioning, decision-making, and repetition. Stocks, bonds, and other investments each play a role, just like defenders, midfielders, and attackers. No single position wins matches alone.

This section will help you understand how the financial markets actually work, how risk and return interact, and how different investments fit together. You will learn why diversification matters, why volatility is normal, and why long-term success depends more on discipline than brilliance.

Buildup investing means trusting the process even when nothing dramatic seems to be happening. It means sticking to fundamentals when emotions try to take over. It means knowing that consistent, well-structured play creates more goals than hero shots ever will.

When your attack is built properly, you do not need to panic. Opportunities come naturally. You recognize them because the system puts you in position to succeed.

That is the mindset this section develops.

Chapter 9: How the Financial Markets Really Work

Financial markets often feel overwhelming to athletes because they never stop moving. Prices update constantly. Headlines shift by the hour. Social media turns every fluctuation into a crisis or an opportunity. From the outside, it can feel like chaos.

In reality, markets are structured systems with rules, incentives, and long-term patterns. They are not random. They are emotional in the short term and logical over time. Once you understand how they actually work, fear fades and decision-making improves.

How Markets Function

At their core, financial markets exist to move capital.

Businesses need money to grow, hire, build, and innovate. Investors provide that capital in exchange for ownership or income. Markets are simply the meeting place where those exchanges occur.

Prices change because expectations change. Earnings reports, economic data, interest rates, and global events all influence how investors collectively view the future. When expectations rise, prices rise. When expectations fall, prices fall.

This does not mean markets are always right in the short term. Emotion plays a major role. Fear, greed, optimism, and panic show up constantly. But over long periods, fundamentals tend to win. Profitable companies that grow tend to increase in value. Weak businesses struggle.

Markets reward patience and understanding. They punish reaction and confusion.

Stocks, Bonds, and Ownership

One of the most important mindset shifts is understanding what you actually own.

When you buy stock, you are buying ownership in a company. You are participating in its future. Revenue growth, profitability, innovation, competition, and management decisions all affect your outcome.

Stocks represent offense. They drive long-term growth. They also come with volatility because ownership means exposure to uncertainty.

Bonds work differently. Bonds represent lending, not ownership. You are loaning money to a government or company in exchange for interest and repayment over time.

Bonds tend to be more stable. They generate income and reduce volatility, but they usually do not grow as fast as stocks over long periods.

Both matter. Stocks push the attack forward. Bonds help maintain shape and stability. Relying on one alone creates imbalance.

Market Cycles and Volatility

Markets move in cycles. Expansion. Slowdown. Contraction. Recovery.

These cycles are normal and unavoidable. Trying to eliminate them is like trying to play a full season without fatigue or injuries. It does not happen.

Volatility is simply movement. It feels uncomfortable because prices go down as well as up. But volatility is not failure. It is part of how markets reset expectations and reprice risk.

Athletes often struggle here because volatility feels like losing. In sports, losing a match has immediate consequences. In investing, short-term declines are part of long-term success.

Problems arise when people treat temporary downturns as permanent damage. Selling during volatility locks in losses. Abandoning strategy turns normal cycles into self-inflicted wounds.

Long-term investors expect volatility and plan for it. Short-term traders try to avoid it or exploit it. One approach builds wealth. The other builds stress.

Long-Term Strategy vs Chasing Form

Chasing form is one of the most common mistakes athletes make with money.

Hot stocks, trending sectors, and viral strategies feel exciting. They promise fast results. They also tend to appear after much of the opportunity has already passed.

In soccer, chasing the ball instead of maintaining shape creates gaps. Financially, chasing performance creates risk.

Long-term strategy focuses on diversification, discipline, and consistency. It accepts that no single investment will always perform best. It spreads risk across assets, sectors, and time.

This approach feels boring. That is why it works.

The market does not reward urgency. It rewards patience and repetition.

Coach's Perspective: What Would Your Coach Say?

Your coach would not want emotional decision-making.

They would say:

Trust the system.

Stay composed.

Play the long game.

Do not chase every ball.

Execute the plan.

Financially, this means ignoring noise, focusing on fundamentals, and letting time do the heavy lifting. Coaches understand that discipline under pressure separates consistent performers from inconsistent ones.

Game Situations and Decision Points

Situation one. Markets drop sharply and headlines turn negative. Do you panic and abandon your plan, or do you stay positioned?

Situation two. A friend or influencer is making money quickly in a hot investment. Do you chase it without context, or evaluate how it fits your system?

Situation three. Progress feels slow and uneventful. Do you force action, or trust the buildup?

Each decision mirrors a moment on the pitch. The wrong choice feels urgent. The right choice feels patient.

Common Athlete Mistakes and Financial Parallels

Athletes mistake movement for opportunity. Markets move constantly, but not every movement matters.

Athletes chase momentum without structure. Markets punish that behavior.

Athletes abandon systems when pressure rises. Markets reward those who stay disciplined.

Athletes trust confidence over preparation. Markets reward preparation every time.

Recognizing these patterns helps you avoid costly mistakes.

Winning the Long Game

Markets are not designed to make you rich quickly. They are designed to reward people who show up consistently, stay disciplined, and think in seasons rather than moments.

Long-term investing is not about predicting the future. It is about positioning yourself so that whatever happens, you remain in the match.

When you understand how markets really work, fear loses its grip. Decisions slow down. Confidence becomes grounded, not emotional.

You stop chasing form. You stop reacting to noise. You start building attacks that develop naturally.

That is how long-term success is created.

Athlete Takeaways

- Markets connect capital and opportunity, not luck and guesses.
- Stocks represent ownership. Bonds represent lending. Both matter.
- Volatility is normal and expected across cycles.
- Long-term strategy beats chasing form, every season.

Chapter 10: Risk, Return, and the Power of Compounding

Every meaningful decision in soccer involves tradeoffs.

Push numbers forward and you increase scoring chances, but you expose yourself defensively. Sit too deep and you reduce risk, but you limit opportunity. The game is a constant balance between attack and protection.

Money works the same way.

Risk and return are permanently connected. You cannot separate them, only manage how much of each you take on and when. Understanding that relationship is what allows compounding to work in your favor instead of against you.

Risk and Reward Tradeoffs

There is no such thing as reward without risk.

Higher potential returns come with higher uncertainty. Lower risk choices usually offer lower growth. This is not unfair. It is how the system stays balanced. If high returns came without risk, everyone would choose them and the advantage would disappear.

Athletes sometimes struggle with this idea because effort and reward are closely linked in sports. Train harder, get better. Do more reps, improve performance. You see the connection between work and results.

Investing does not respond to effort the same way. You cannot outwork the market. Watching prices more often does not increase returns. Stressing harder does not improve outcomes.

What you can do is choose appropriate risk.

Risk should match your timeline, goals, and flexibility. Money needed soon should not be exposed to high volatility. Money meant for long term growth can handle more ups and downs because time absorbs shocks.

Problems arise when people take risks they do not understand or cannot afford. When outcomes go against them, panic replaces planning. They abandon strategy at the worst possible time.

Smart investing accepts risk intentionally. It does not chase reward blindly.

Volatility vs Permanent Loss

Volatility feels like losing. Permanent loss actually is.

Volatility is movement. Prices rise and fall. Values fluctuate. This is normal and unavoidable in markets that are constantly pricing the future. News, expectations, and uncertainty create short term swings.

Permanent loss happens when capital is destroyed or removed from the game. Selling during downturns. Concentrating too heavily in one idea that fails. Taking risks that force you out at the wrong time. These actions lock in damage.

Athletes often confuse the two because both feel uncomfortable.

In soccer, conceding a goal feels bad, but it does not end the match. A red card or serious injury can. Volatility is the conceded goal. Permanent loss is being unable to continue playing the game.

Markets have historically recovered over time. Many individual investors do not, because decisions made during volatility turn temporary setbacks into permanent losses.

Understanding this difference changes behavior. You stop reacting to every swing and start protecting your ability to stay invested. Staying in the match matters more than winning every moment.

Compounding Over Time

Compounding is the most powerful force in investing, and the most underestimated.

Compounding is growth building on top of growth. Returns earn returns. Progress accelerates quietly. Early on, it looks small. Later, it becomes significant.

It does not look impressive at first. In fact, it often feels slow and underwhelming. The early years require patience because the math is still warming up.

Athletes understand this from training. Early gains are slow. Strength, endurance, and skill build gradually. Over time, consistent work produces noticeable change. Skip sessions or quit early and the payoff never arrives.

Compounding requires three things. Time. Consistency. Discipline.

Time allows growth to build on itself.

Consistency keeps money working regularly.

Discipline prevents emotional decisions that interrupt the process.

Miss any one of these and results shrink dramatically. The market does not reward intensity. It rewards staying in position long enough for compounding to work.

The Hidden Cost of Waiting

Waiting feels safe. It often feels responsible.

Many athletes delay investing because they want more certainty. More income. Better timing. Less risk. They tell themselves they will start later when things feel more stable.

The cost of waiting is invisible, but real.

Every year you delay is a year compounding does not work for you. Time is not replaceable. You cannot add it back later with bigger contributions or smarter moves. Starting earlier with smaller amounts often beats starting later with larger ones.

This does not mean rushing or taking inappropriate risk. It means recognizing that perfect conditions never arrive. There will always be uncertainty. There will always be headlines. There will always be reasons to wait.

In soccer, waiting too long to make a pass closes the window. Financially, waiting too long delays growth.

Starting small, early, and consistently beats starting big, late, and sporadic.

Coach's Perspective: What Would Your Coach Say?

Your coach would not want fear-based decisions.

They would say:

Trust the work.

Stay patient.

Do not flinch.

Play the long game.

Control what you can control.

Financially, that means choosing appropriate risk, staying disciplined through volatility, and giving compounding time to do its job. You control savings rate, diversification, and behavior. You do not control short term market moves.

Coaches know that success is built through consistency, not desperation.

Game Situations and Decision Points

Situation one. Markets drop and volatility spikes.

Do you panic and exit, or do you stay positioned according to your plan? Short term discomfort often leads to long term mistakes.

Situation two. You want higher returns quickly.

Do you take risks you cannot afford, or accept steady progress? Chasing shortcuts often increases the chance of permanent loss.

Situation three. You delay investing while waiting for certainty.

Do you recognize what that delay costs over time? Safety today can mean opportunity lost tomorrow.

Each decision affects whether compounding works for you or against you.

Common Athlete Mistakes and Financial Parallels

Athletes mistake comfort for safety. Waiting feels safe but can be costly.

Athletes chase upside without protection. Money punishes imbalance.

Athletes react emotionally to setbacks. Markets reward emotional control.

Athletes underestimate time. Compounding depends on it.

Recognizing these patterns helps you stay in the match long enough for progress to build.

Winning the Long Game

Risk is not the enemy. Mismanaged risk is.

Compounding rewards those who stay disciplined, stay invested, and stay patient. It punishes those who chase excitement, react emotionally, or wait indefinitely.

Financial success is rarely dramatic. It is quiet, gradual, and built over years of steady decisions.

When you understand risk, return, and compounding, you stop forcing plays. You let the system work. You focus on positioning, not headlines.

That is how long careers are built. That is how wealth compounds.

Athlete Takeaways

Risk and reward are linked. Choose risk intentionally.

Volatility is normal. Permanent loss is the real danger.

Compounding rewards time, consistency, and discipline.

Waiting has a cost. Start early and stay positioned.

Chapter 11: Stocks Without the Transfer Rumors

Stocks get a bad reputation among athletes because they are often talked about the wrong way.

Instead of being explained as ownership in real businesses, stocks are discussed like transfer rumors. Who is hot. Who is about to break out. Who everyone is talking about right now. The conversation becomes speculation instead of understanding.

That mindset leads to poor decisions.

This chapter is about stripping away the noise and understanding what stocks actually are, how different styles of investing work, and why long-term ownership beats rumor chasing every time.

What Owning Stock Actually Means

When you buy a stock, you are not betting on a price. You are buying ownership in a company.

That company sells products or services. It hires employees. It competes. It makes profits or losses. As an owner, your results are tied to how that business performs over time.

This is an important shift in thinking.

Stock prices move every day, but businesses do not change every day. Long-term investors focus on business fundamentals, not short-term price swings.

If a company grows revenue, manages costs, innovates, and stays competitive, ownership tends to become more valuable over time. If it fails to do those things, ownership loses value.

Stocks are not lottery tickets. They are ownership stakes in real economic activity.

Growth vs Value Investing

Growth and value investing are two common ways people describe stocks.

Growth investing focuses on companies expected to grow faster than average. These businesses often reinvest profits to expand, innovate, or capture market share. They may not pay much income today because they are focused on tomorrow.

Value investing focuses on companies that appear undervalued relative to their fundamentals. These businesses may be established, profitable, and steady, but temporarily out of favor.

Neither approach is superior in all conditions.

Growth can outperform when innovation and expansion are rewarded. Value can outperform when stability and cash flow matter more.

Athletes often gravitate toward growth because it sounds exciting. Fast. Dynamic. High upside. The mistake is assuming growth always wins.

Smart portfolios usually include both. Just like a balanced squad needs youth and experience, speed and composure.

Dividends and Total Return

Dividends are cash payments companies make to shareholders.

Some investors focus heavily on dividends because they feel tangible. Money shows up in the account. It feels like scoring.

Dividends can be useful, but they are only part of the picture.

Total return includes both price appreciation and dividends. A stock that grows steadily without paying dividends can outperform a high-dividend stock over time. Likewise, dividends reinvested can compound powerfully.

Chasing dividends alone can lead to missed opportunities. Ignoring them entirely can also be a mistake.

The goal is not one type of return. It is total progress over time.

Common Investing Myths

There are several myths that trap athletes.

One myth is that stock investing is just gambling. Gambling relies on luck. Investing relies on ownership, diversification, and time. They are not the same.

Another myth is that you need to time the market perfectly. You do not. Trying to buy at the bottom and sell at the top usually leads to missed opportunities and emotional mistakes.

Another myth is that you need insider information to succeed. You do not. Public markets already reflect known information. Discipline matters more than secrets.

A final myth is that successful investing is exciting. It is not. The best strategies are often boring, repetitive, and quiet.

Coach's Perspective: What Would Your Coach Say?

Your coach would shut down rumor-driven decisions.

They would say:

Focus on fundamentals.

Trust the system.

Do not chase noise.

Play your role.

Be consistent.

Financially, that means understanding what you own, why you own it, and how it fits your plan. Not reacting to headlines or hype.

Game Situations and Decision Points

Situation one. A stock is all over social media. Do you buy without understanding the business, or do you pass?

Situation two. A solid investment is underperforming temporarily. Do you panic, or remember why you owned it?

Situation three. Your portfolio feels boring. Do you force action, or trust discipline?

Each moment tests patience and perspective.

Common Athlete Mistakes and Financial Parallels

Athletes chase hype instead of fundamentals. Markets punish that behavior.

Athletes confuse excitement with effectiveness. Money rewards consistency.

Athletes follow the crowd. Investing requires independent thinking.

Athletes abandon plans under pressure. Markets reward staying power.

Winning the Long Game

Owning stocks is about believing in long-term progress, not predicting short-term headlines.

When you understand stocks as ownership, decisions slow down. Emotions settle. Discipline increases.

You stop chasing rumors and start building real value.

That is how wealth is built quietly over time.

Athlete Takeaways

- Stocks represent ownership in real businesses, not bets.
- Growth and value both matter across cycles.
- Dividends are part of total return, not the whole story.
- Ignore transfer rumors. Trust fundamentals and discipline.

Chapter 12: Bonds and Controlling the Midfield

Every strong soccer team has a midfield that keeps things calm when the match gets chaotic.

Midfielders control tempo. They recycle possession. They connect defense to attack. They help the team breathe when pressure builds. They do not always get the glory, but without them, the team loses shape and control.

Bonds play that same role in a portfolio.

They are not designed to score highlight goals. They are designed to stabilize the match, manage risk, and keep you from losing control when conditions turn against you. When markets get chaotic, bonds help you keep structure instead of scrambling.

How Bonds Work

At their simplest, bonds are loans.

When you buy a bond, you are lending money to a government, municipality, or company. In return, you receive interest payments and the promise that your original amount, called principal, will be returned at a future date known as maturity.

This is different from stocks. Stocks represent ownership. You share in profits and growth, but also in uncertainty. Bonds represent obligation. The issuer owes you scheduled payments.

The bond issuer agrees to pay you interest for using your money. The bond holder accepts lower growth potential in exchange for greater predictability.

Bonds come with timelines. Some mature in a few months. Others last years or even decades. As bonds approach maturity, their value becomes more predictable, assuming the issuer can meet its obligations. That approaching maturity acts like the clock running down in a match. The outcome becomes clearer.

This predictability is why bonds are often described as safer than stocks. Safer does not mean risk free. It means the role they play is different. They are designed to reduce swings, not maximize upside.

Interest Rate and Credit Risk

Two primary risks affect bonds: interest rate risk and credit risk.

Interest rate risk refers to how bond prices react when interest rates change. When rates rise, existing bonds become less attractive because new bonds are issued with higher yields. As a result, prices of older bonds fall. When rates fall, existing bonds paying higher rates become more valuable.

This does not mean bonds are broken. It means their market value adjusts to the environment. Over time, bonds continue to pay interest and move toward maturity.

Credit risk refers to the issuer's ability to repay the loan. Governments, large corporations, and financially stable institutions generally carry lower credit risk. Smaller or financially weaker issuers carry higher risk and therefore must offer higher interest to attract investors.

Higher yields always come with a reason.

Athletes sometimes chase higher yields without understanding the tradeoff. It feels like a scoring opportunity, but it may come with hidden exposure. Just like pressing aggressively without support, it can work briefly, but it leaves space behind you.

Understanding these risks helps you choose bonds that fit your role in the lineup rather than chasing numbers alone.

When Bonds Make Sense

Bonds make sense when stability matters.

They become more important as time horizons shorten, responsibilities grow, or flexibility decreases. Money needed in the near future cannot afford wild swings. Tuition, a home purchase, or retirement withdrawals require reliability.

Bonds also matter psychologically.

Even disciplined athletes can struggle when markets fall sharply. Watching only stock values drop can create emotional pressure that leads to poor decisions. Seeing part of your portfolio hold steady can provide confidence to stay disciplined.

Bonds are not about maximizing returns. They are about managing behavior and protecting progress. They help prevent panic selling, which turns temporary volatility into permanent loss.

They often play a larger role as you approach retirement, major purchases, or periods when income becomes less predictable.

You do not add midfielders because you are afraid to score. You add them because control wins matches.

Stability in a Diversified Portfolio

Diversification is about combining assets that behave differently.

Stocks and bonds often respond differently to economic conditions. When stocks struggle due to uncertainty or market stress, bonds may hold steady or even rise, especially high-quality bonds. When stocks perform well, bonds may lag but provide balance.

This relationship smooths outcomes. It does not eliminate downturns, but it reduces the severity of swings.

A portfolio without bonds can feel like playing with too many attackers. It looks exciting when everything goes well, but collapses quickly when momentum shifts. There is no structure to slow the game down.

Stability does not mean stagnation. It means staying in the match long enough for your strategy to work. Bonds give portfolios time and space to breathe.

Coach's Perspective: What Would Your Coach Say?

Your coach would respect balance.

They would say:

Control the tempo.

Keep your shape.

Do not force it.

Make the simple play.

Stay connected.

Financially, that means using bonds to manage risk, not chase excitement. It means understanding their role and trusting them to do their job even when they are not producing highlight moments.

Good teams win because they stay organized under pressure. Good portfolios survive because they are structured for different conditions.

Game Situations and Decision Points

Situation one. Markets are volatile and emotions are high.

Do you panic and sell, or rely on the stability in your portfolio to stay composed?

Situation two. You feel bonds are boring compared to stocks.

Do you remove them to chase more excitement, or respect the role they play in protecting your overall plan?

Situation three. Your time horizon shortens because of life changes or upcoming goals.

Do you adjust risk accordingly, or pretend nothing changed?

Each choice affects control. Control often matters more than speed.

Common Athlete Mistakes and Financial Parallels

Athletes undervalue midfield play. Portfolios collapse without balance.

Athletes chase speed and flash. Money rewards structure and patience.

Athletes abandon shape under pressure. Markets punish that behavior.

Athletes forget the role of defense and connection. Long term success requires both.

Recognizing these patterns prevents overexposure and helps you maintain composure when conditions are difficult.

Winning the Long Game

Bonds are not designed to excite you. They are designed to protect you.

They help you stay disciplined during downturns. They reduce volatility. They allow you to make rational decisions when others panic.

Just like midfield control wins championships, portfolio stability supports long careers. You do not notice bonds much when everything is going well. You appreciate them most when conditions turn difficult.

That is their value. Quiet control when the game speeds up.

Athlete Takeaways

Bonds are loans that provide stability, not ownership.

Interest rate and credit risk shape how bonds behave.

Bonds matter more as timelines shorten and responsibilities grow.

Stability keeps you in the match long enough to win.

Control of the midfield, and the portfolio, is what allows strategy to succeed.

Chapter 13: Funds, ETFs, and Team-Based Investing

No soccer team wins consistently with one great player and nothing else.

Championship teams are built on depth, balance, and roles. Everyone does not need to score. Everyone needs to contribute. When one player has an off day, the system still works.

Funds and ETFs exist for the same reason. They allow you to invest as a team instead of relying on individual stars.

This chapter is about understanding how team-based investing works, why it reduces unnecessary risk, and how you can build diversification without turning investing into a second full-time job.

Mutual Funds vs ETFs

Mutual funds and ETFs both pool money from many investors to buy a collection of investments.

Instead of owning one stock or bond, you own a slice of many. This immediately reduces risk and complexity.

The main difference is how they trade and how they are structured.

Mutual funds are typically bought and sold at the end of the day at a single price. You place an order, and the transaction happens after markets close. Many employer retirement plans use mutual funds because they are easy to administer and automate.

ETFs trade throughout the day like stocks. Prices move in real time. You can buy or sell whenever the market is open. ETFs often have lower fees and more flexibility, which is why they have become increasingly popular.

From a long-term perspective, both can work. The choice is less about which is "better" and more about cost, access, and how you plan to use them.

The mistake athletes make is assuming structure matters more than discipline. It does not.

A simple fund used consistently beats a complex structure used inconsistently.

Index vs Active Strategies

Index investing means owning a fund that simply tracks a market or segment of the market. No predictions. No stock picking. No opinions.

The fund owns everything in the index and adjusts automatically as the market changes.

Active investing means a manager is trying to outperform the market by selecting specific investments. Sometimes this works. Often it does not.

Index strategies appeal to athletes because they are rules-based and consistent. There is a system. It does not change based on emotion. It executes the same way every season.

Active strategies appeal because they promise an edge. The problem is that edges are hard to maintain, expensive, and unpredictable.

Over long periods, many active strategies fail to outperform after fees. That does not mean active investing is useless. It means it should be used intentionally, not assumed to be superior.

Just like in soccer, systems beat individual brilliance more often than people want to admit.

Fees and Expense Ratios

Fees are the silent opponent most investors underestimate.

Expense ratios are the annual costs charged by funds. They may look small. A fraction of a percent. But over time, they compound in the wrong direction.

A fund with higher fees has to outperform just to keep up. Many never do.

Athletes understand this concept instinctively. Small mistakes repeated every match become big problems over a season. Fees work the same way.

Lower fees do not guarantee better returns, but high fees guarantee a headwind.

This does not mean choosing the cheapest option blindly. It means understanding what you are paying for and whether it actually adds value.

Most long-term success comes from controlling what you can control. Fees are controllable.

Diversification Without Complexity

Diversification is often misunderstood.

It does not mean owning everything. It means owning enough different assets so that no single failure ruins the plan.

Funds and ETFs make this easy.

One fund can give exposure to hundreds or thousands of companies. Another can balance risk with bonds. Together, they create structure without constant decision-making.

Athletes often overcomplicate investing because they think more activity equals better results. In reality, simplicity improves consistency.

A diversified portfolio does not need frequent changes. It needs periodic review and discipline.

This is team-based investing at its best. Each position plays a role. No one player carries the entire load.

Coach's Perspective: What Would Your Coach Say?

Your coach would not want hero ball.

They would say:

Trust the system.

Everyone has a role.

Depth wins seasons.

Do your job.

Play within the structure.

Financially, that means using diversified funds to reduce risk, manage emotion, and stay disciplined.

Good teams are boring to play against because they do not beat themselves.

Game Situations and Decision Points

Situation one. You are tempted to invest heavily in one stock you believe in. Do you rely on one player, or build a team?

Situation two. You see a fund with higher fees but impressive marketing. Do you evaluate substance or chase promises?

Situation three. Your portfolio feels quiet. Do you force changes, or trust diversification?

Each decision tests discipline.

Common Athlete Mistakes and Financial Parallels

Athletes overvalue stars. Portfolios collapse without depth.

Athletes chase confidence over consistency. Money rewards systems.

Athletes mistake complexity for sophistication. Simplicity scales better.

Athletes change strategy too often. Reps matter in investing too.

Recognizing these patterns keeps you in control.

Winning the Long Game

Funds and ETFs are not about excitement. They are about reliability.

They reduce the need for perfect decisions. They smooth outcomes. They help you stay invested through volatility.

Team-based investing wins because it removes ego from the process.

You stop trying to predict outcomes and start executing a plan.

That is how long-term success is built.

Athlete Takeaways

- Funds and ETFs let you invest as a team, not as a solo act.
- Index strategies provide discipline and consistency across cycles.
- Fees compound against you. Control them.
- Diversification works best when it is simple and repeatable.

Chapter 14: Real Estate and Alternative Plays

Real estate and alternative investments attract athletes because they feel tangible, different, and separate from the stock market. You can see a building. You can touch land. You can point to something and say, "I own that."

That feeling of control is powerful. It can also be misleading.

This chapter is about understanding where real estate and alternative investments actually fit, what tradeoffs they introduce, and how to think about them as part of a bigger system rather than standalone plays.

Renting vs Owning

Renting and owning are not moral decisions. They are strategic ones.

Renting buys flexibility. You pay for shelter without committing capital, maintenance, or long-term responsibility. This matters when income is uncertain, careers are changing, or mobility is important.

Owning buys stability and control. You lock in housing costs, build equity over time, and reduce uncertainty around where you live. Ownership can be powerful when you plan to stay put and can comfortably handle the costs.

Athletes often rush into ownership because it feels like progress. In reality, buying too early or too aggressively can create pressure.

Ownership comes with hidden responsibilities. Repairs. Taxes. Insurance. Illiquidity. These costs do not show up in the listing price.

The right question is not "Should I own?" It is "Does owning fit my current stage and flexibility?"

Just like in soccer, timing matters. Making the right move at the wrong time still causes problems.

REITs and Indirect Ownership

Real estate investment trusts, often called REITs, allow you to invest in real estate without owning property directly.

REITs own collections of buildings like apartments, offices, warehouses, healthcare facilities, or retail spaces. When you invest, you own a slice of that portfolio.

This structure offers several advantages. Diversification across many properties. Professional management. Liquidity, since many REITs trade like stocks.

For athletes, REITs can provide real estate exposure without the headaches of tenants, repairs, or large capital commitments.

The tradeoff is control. You cannot choose the properties. You cannot make individual decisions. You are trusting the system instead of running the operation yourself.

REITs are not replacements for direct ownership. They are tools. Used correctly, they add balance. Used incorrectly, they are misunderstood.

Alternatives Like Commodities and Private Investments

Alternative investments include things like commodities, private equity, private real estate deals, venture investments, and collectibles.

These assets often sound sophisticated and exclusive. They are marketed as ways to diversify beyond traditional markets.

Some alternatives can play a useful role. Others introduce risk without clear benefit.

Commodities can hedge certain risks, but they often produce no income and rely heavily on price movement. Private investments can offer high upside, but they come with high failure rates and limited transparency.

Athletes are frequently targeted with private opportunities because of their networks and perceived access. The language often emphasizes scarcity, urgency, and insider status.

Those are warning signs.

Alternatives require deeper understanding, longer timelines, and higher risk tolerance. They are not substitutes for a strong foundation.

In soccer terms, these are specialty roles, not core positions. You do not build a lineup around them.

Liquidity and Risk Considerations

Liquidity is how quickly you can access your money without major loss.

Stocks and many bonds are liquid. You can sell them quickly. Real estate and alternatives are not.

Illiquidity is not bad. It just needs to be intentional.

When money is locked up, you lose flexibility. That matters if income changes, opportunities arise, or emergencies occur.

Athletes often underestimate this risk. A portfolio full of illiquid investments looks impressive until cash is needed quickly.

Risk also shows up differently in these assets. Valuations may not update daily. That can feel comforting, but it does not eliminate risk. It just hides volatility.

Understanding liquidity keeps you from overcommitting to assets that limit options.

Coach's Perspective: What Would Your Coach Say?

Your coach would not want forced plays.

They would say:

Know the situation.

Do not overcommit.

Play within your role.

Balance the lineup.

Protect flexibility.

Financially, that means using real estate and alternatives thoughtfully, not emotionally. Making sure the core system stays intact.

Good teams know when to build and when to hold shape.

Game Situations and Decision Points

Situation one. You feel pressure to buy property because everyone else is. Do you evaluate fit, or chase status?

Situation two. A private deal promises high returns. Do you understand the risks, or trust the pitch?

Situation three. Most of your money becomes illiquid. Do you still have flexibility?

Each decision affects future options.

Common Athlete Mistakes and Financial Parallels

Athletes confuse ownership with success. Money requires alignment, not symbols.

Athletes underestimate recovery time. Illiquid assets lock you in longer than expected.

Athletes trust access over analysis. Markets punish that behavior.

Athletes chase uniqueness. Long-term success favors fundamentals.

Recognizing these mistakes prevents overexposure.

Winning the Long Game

Real estate and alternative investments are tools, not trophies.

They can strengthen a portfolio when used correctly. They can weaken it when overused or misunderstood.

The goal is balance. Growth without rigidity. Ownership without pressure. Opportunity without desperation.

When these assets fit your system, they add depth. When they do not, they create risk.

Smart investing is not about doing everything. It is about doing the right things at the right time.

Athlete Takeaways

- Renting and owning are strategic choices, not status markers.
- REITs offer real estate exposure without operational burden.
- Alternatives require higher risk tolerance and longer timelines.
- Liquidity matters. Flexibility keeps you in the match.

Part IV: Managing the Match (Portfolio Management)

Winning requires adjustments, not panic substitutions.

Great teams are not defined by how they start matches. They are defined by how they manage them.

As the game unfolds, conditions change. Momentum swings. Fatigue sets in. Opponents adjust. The best teams respond calmly. They make thoughtful adjustments, not emotional ones. They trust the game plan while staying flexible enough to adapt.

Portfolio management works the same way.

Building a portfolio is only the beginning. Managing it over time is where success or failure shows up. Markets change. Life changes. Goals evolve. The challenge is knowing when to make adjustments and when to stay the course.

Most investing mistakes happen here.

Panic substitutions feel productive. Selling after losses. Buying after rallies. Overreacting to headlines. Making changes to feel in control. These moves rarely improve outcomes. They usually lock in mistakes.

Smart portfolio management is quieter.

It is about reviewing, not reacting. Adjusting when circumstances change, not when emotions spike. Making small, disciplined moves that keep the overall system intact.

Just like soccer, not every moment calls for a substitution. Sometimes the best move is to settle the team, slow the tempo, and let the plan work.

This section focuses on how to manage investments across seasons, not moments. Asset allocation, buying and holding, rebalancing, and mental discipline are the tools that keep you competitive over the long run.

Winning does not require constant action. It requires the right action at the right time.

The goal is not to predict every twist in the match. The goal is to stay composed, stay organized, and finish strong.

Chapter 15: Asset Allocation and Squad Selection

Winning teams are built before kickoff.

Coaches spend countless hours deciding who starts, who comes off the bench, and how roles fit together. Squad selection is not about picking the most talented individuals. It is about balance, chemistry, depth, and understanding the match you are trying to win.

A team full of attackers looks impressive on paper but falls apart under pressure. A team built only for defense struggles to score. Great teams are built for different game states. Leading, trailing, under pressure, or in control.

Asset allocation is the same idea applied to money.

It is not about finding the best investment. It is about deciding how much to put in each type of investment so the whole system works together across different conditions.

Stocks, Bonds, and Cash Balance

Every portfolio needs multiple roles.

Stocks are your attackers.

They drive growth. They create long-term opportunity. They are how wealth expands over time. But offense always carries risk. Stocks can be volatile, and short-term results are unpredictable.

Bonds are your midfielders and defenders.

They manage tempo, reduce swings, and provide stability when conditions get rough. They do not usually produce the highest returns, but they help protect the structure of the team.

Cash is your goalkeeper.

It does not generate excitement. It does not score goals. But when something unexpected happens, job loss, medical expense, market downturn, cash keeps you in the match. It provides immediate flexibility and prevents forced decisions.

Problems arise when portfolios lean too heavily in one direction.

All offense means big swings and emotional pressure. It looks great in strong markets but becomes stressful during downturns. All defense means limited growth and missed opportunity. Too much cash means safety without progress, which can quietly erode purchasing power over time.

Balance depends on goals and timelines. Long-term money can handle more stocks because time absorbs volatility. Short-term needs require more bonds and cash because reliability matters more than growth.

Asset allocation is not about maximizing returns in any single year. It is about surviving every year so progress can compound.

Domestic vs International Exposure

Many athletes invest only in what feels familiar. Domestic companies. Domestic markets. Brands they recognize. It feels safer because it feels known.

The global economy does not work that way.

Opportunities exist everywhere. Different countries grow at different speeds. Different regions lead at different times. Economic cycles do not move in perfect sync across the world.

Concentrating only at home limits diversification. It ties your outcome to one system, one set of policies, one currency environment.

International exposure spreads risk. When one market struggles, another may perform better. This does not eliminate volatility, but it smooths outcomes over time and increases the number of growth engines working for you.

Global diversification is like having depth across competitions. League play, tournaments, international matches. You are not dependent on one environment to succeed.

Ignoring international exposure is not automatically reckless, but it is incomplete. A global game deserves a global roster.

Diversification Principles

Diversification is often misunderstood.

It is not about owning everything. It is about owning enough different things so that no single outcome ruins the plan.

True diversification happens across asset types, regions, industries, and time. It means combining investments that respond differently to economic conditions.

Buying many similar investments does not count. Owning five technology stocks is still one bet. Owning different types of assets that move differently under pressure is real diversification.

Diversification does not guarantee profits. It reduces the risk of catastrophic failure. It lowers the chance that one mistake or one bad cycle derails your entire strategy.

In soccer terms, diversification is depth and shape. If one player struggles, the team adapts. If one investment underperforms, the portfolio absorbs it.

This is how consistency is built, not through perfect prediction, but through smart structure.

Career-Stage Allocation

Asset allocation should change as your life changes.

Early career often allows for more risk. Time is on your side. Income potential is growing. Volatility matters less because there is time to recover and add more money over the years.

Mid-career brings more responsibilities. Family, housing, lifestyle commitments, and career stability become priorities. Allocation often becomes more balanced to protect progress while still allowing growth.

Later career and retirement focus more on preservation and income. The role of the portfolio shifts from accumulation to supporting spending. Risk shifts from maximizing growth to sustaining what has been built.

The mistake athletes make is freezing allocation in one stage. What worked at 22 may be dangerous at 42. What feels safe later may have been inefficient earlier.

Asset allocation is dynamic. It evolves with your role in the match and the stage of your season.

Coach's Perspective: What Would Your Coach Say?

Your coach would emphasize balance and fit.

They would say:

Play to your strengths.

Know your role.

Balance the lineup.

Protect the team shape.

Think long term.

Financially, that means choosing allocation based on your timeline, responsibilities, and goals, not emotion or headlines. Great coaches build squads that can handle different game states, not just ideal conditions.

Game Situations and Decision Points

Situation one. Markets are volatile and fear rises.

Do you abandon offense completely or trust the balance in your structure?

Situation two. One asset class is dominating performance.

Do you overload that position or maintain shape and discipline?

Situation three. Life changes. Marriage, kids, career shifts.

Do you adjust allocation or ignore reality and hope the old plan still works?

Each decision affects long-term control and the ability to stay consistent.

Common Athlete Mistakes and Financial Parallels

Athletes chase highlight performances. Portfolios need consistency.

Athletes overvalue stars. Teams need balance across roles.

Athletes ignore depth. Money punishes concentration.

Athletes resist adjustment. Long seasons and long lives require flexibility.

Recognizing these patterns keeps the system intact when conditions change.

Winning the Long Game

Asset allocation is not exciting. That is exactly why it works.

It removes pressure from individual decisions. It allows you to stay disciplined when markets move unpredictably. It keeps progress intact across seasons, cycles, and life stages.

You do not need perfect picks. You need a squad that works together.

When allocation is right, you stop reacting to every headline and start managing with intention. You trust the system. You make small adjustments instead of big mistakes.

That is how championships are built. That is how financial success lasts.

Athlete Takeaways

Stocks grow. Bonds stabilize. Cash protects. Balance matters.

Global exposure spreads risk beyond familiar ground.

Diversification prevents one mistake from ending the season.

Allocation should evolve as your career and life change.

Strong squads, and strong portfolios, win over the long season.

Chapter 16: Buying, Holding, and Trusting the System

Every team has a system.

You train it. You drill it. You repeat it until decisions become automatic. On match day, the system exists so you do not have to think through every moment from scratch. Under pressure, you rely on preparation, not improvisation.

Investing works the same way.

Buying, holding, and trusting the system is not about brilliance. It is about removing emotion, reducing mistakes, and letting preparation do its job over time. Most people do not fail because their system is bad. They fail because they abandon it when pressure rises.

Opening and Funding Accounts

Before anything else, the system has to exist.

Opening investment accounts is like registering for the season. You can talk about strategy all you want, but nothing counts until you are officially in the game.

Retirement accounts, brokerage accounts, employer plans, each serves a role. Some offer tax advantages. Some provide flexibility. The specific account matters, but not as much as actually starting and using it consistently.

Funding the account is where discipline begins.

One-time deposits help. Regular contributions change outcomes. The habit of contributing matters more than the size at the beginning.

Automated contributions remove hesitation. They turn investing into a routine instead of a recurring decision. Just like showing up to training, consistency beats intensity. You do not need a perfect session every day. You need repeated sessions over time.

Athletes often wait until they feel ready. More income. More certainty. Better timing. That delay costs reps.

You do not wait to train until you feel perfect. You train to improve. Investing works the same way.

Market Orders vs Limit Orders

Execution matters, but not as much as people think.

A market order buys or sells immediately at the current price. It prioritizes getting the trade done. A limit order sets a specific price and waits. It prioritizes price over timing.

For long-term investors, the difference between small price changes on a single trade is usually minor compared to the impact of staying invested for years. Obsessing over perfect entry points often causes more harm than good. Missed opportunities, hesitation, and second-guessing add up.

Athletes understand this instinctively. You do not pass up open shots because the angle is not perfect. You take good opportunities when they are available. Waiting for perfect often means missing good.

Precision matters less than participation.

Buy-and-Hold Discipline

Buy-and-hold sounds simple. It is not easy.

Holding through volatility requires trust. Trust in the system. Trust in time. Trust that short-term noise does not invalidate long-term plans.

Markets will test this constantly.

There will be downturns. Headlines will be dramatic. Other people will panic. Your emotions will try to convince you that this time is different and that action is required.

Buy-and-hold discipline means staying positioned even when discomfort rises. It means understanding that volatility is expected and temporary, while abandoning the system can create permanent damage.

Athletes know this lesson from training cycles. Progress is not linear. There are plateaus. There are setbacks. Some days feel terrible. Quitting mid-cycle guarantees failure. Staying consistent gives the process a chance to work.

Holding is the rep most people skip.

Avoiding Emotional Decisions

Emotion is the biggest opponent in investing.

Fear pushes people out at the wrong time. Greed pulls people in too late. Confidence turns into overconfidence. Doubt turns into paralysis.

The system exists to protect you from yourself.

Automation, allocation, and rebalancing are tools that reduce the need for emotional decisions. They set rules in advance so you are not making major choices in the middle of stress.

The less often you feel the need to act, the better long-term outcomes tend to be.

This does not mean ignoring information. It means filtering it. Most news is noise. Most opinions are short-term. Long-term systems do not change because of daily headlines.

Emotion makes people feel productive. Discipline produces results.

Coach's Perspective: What Would Your Coach Say?

Your coach would not want improvisation under pressure.

They would say:

Trust the work.

Stick to the plan.

Next play.

Do not flinch.

Execute.

Financially, that means following through. Buying consistently. Holding patiently. Not abandoning the system because of temporary discomfort.

Coaches know that systems fail when players stop trusting them. The breakdown usually happens mentally before it happens physically.

Game Situations and Decision Points

Situation one. Markets drop and fear spreads.

Do you sell to feel relief, or stay positioned according to your plan? Relief now can mean regret later.

Situation two. Markets surge and excitement rises.

Do you chase more risk because it feels good, or stick to your allocation? Momentum can tempt you away from structure.

Situation three. Progress feels boring.

Do you force action to feel involved, or let the system work quietly? Boredom is often a sign that things are functioning correctly.

Each moment tests discipline more than intelligence.

Common Athlete Mistakes and Financial Parallels

Athletes press when tired. Investors act when emotional.

Athletes abandon structure chasing moments. Investors chase headlines.

Athletes confuse confidence with control. Markets punish that mistake.

Athletes skip fundamentals once they feel comfortable. Investing collapses without them.

Recognizing these patterns keeps you grounded when pressure builds.

Winning the Long Game

Buying and holding is not about being passive. It is about being intentional.

You choose the system. You commit to it. You let time and consistency do the work. You intervene only when your life, goals, or allocation truly change, not because markets moved this week.

The hardest part of investing is not choosing what to buy. It is choosing not to interfere once the plan is in motion.

When you trust the system, decisions simplify. Stress drops. Outcomes improve. You stop reacting to every moment and start managing the season.

That is how long seasons are won. That is how wealth is built quietly over time.

Athlete Takeaways

Start early and fund accounts consistently. Reps matter.

Execution details matter less than participation over time.

Holding through volatility is where results are earned.

Systems exist to protect you from emotional mistakes.

Discipline beats emotion over the long run.

Chapter 17: Halftime Adjustments and Rebalancing

Halftime is not about panic. It is about clarity.

Good teams do not rip up the game plan after one bad half. They review what is actually happening, make targeted adjustments, and return to the pitch composed. They separate emotion from information.

Bad teams overreact. They chase fixes. They substitute emotion for strategy. They make so many changes that no one knows the plan anymore.

Rebalancing plays the same role in investing.

It is the process of bringing your portfolio back into alignment with your original plan as markets move and life changes. Done correctly, it keeps risk under control and decisions disciplined. Done poorly, it turns investing into constant tinkering, stress, and unnecessary mistakes.

This chapter is about knowing when to adjust, how to adjust, and when to leave things alone.

How Often to Review Investments

Reviewing and reacting are not the same thing.

Many investors check their accounts constantly and confuse awareness with action. Every market move feels like a signal. Anxiety rises. Decisions follow emotions instead of strategy.

Others avoid looking at all and hope everything works out. That can lead to neglect, drift, and missed adjustments when they actually matter.

Most long-term investors benefit from scheduled reviews. Once or twice a year is often enough. This creates structure and removes emotion from the process. You review because it is time, not because markets moved.

A review answers simple questions:

Has anything drifted meaningfully from the plan?

Has my life changed?

Has my risk tolerance shifted?

It is not about judging short-term performance. One bad quarter does not invalidate a long-term strategy. Just like one rough half does not define a match.

Regular reviews create confidence. Constant monitoring creates anxiety.

Rebalancing Strategies

Rebalancing is bringing your portfolio back to its intended shape.

Over time, some investments grow faster than others. Stocks may outpace bonds. One region may outperform another. Without adjustment, the portfolio slowly drifts into a different risk profile than you originally intended.

For example, a portfolio that started balanced can quietly become more aggressive after a strong stock run. That might feel good, but it also increases downside risk.

Rebalancing means trimming what has grown too large and adding to what has lagged. This feels uncomfortable because it requires doing the opposite of emotion. Selling what looks good. Buying what feels disappointing.

But this discipline is the point. Rebalancing forces you to "buy low and sell high" in a structured way, not based on feelings.

There are different ways to rebalance. Some investors do it on a schedule, such as once per year. Others rebalance when allocations drift beyond certain ranges, like when a position moves more than a set percentage away from target.

Both approaches work if applied consistently.

Rebalancing is not about predicting what will do well next. It is about restoring balance so the system continues to function as designed.

Life Changes and Portfolio Updates

Markets are not the only reason to adjust.

Life changes matter more.

New job. Marriage. Kids. Home purchase. Business ownership. Health changes. These events affect income, expenses, timelines, and risk capacity.

Ignoring life changes is one of the most common mistakes athletes make with money. They keep the same approach even though their responsibilities and flexibility have changed. What was appropriate earlier may be too aggressive or too conservative now.

A portfolio should reflect your current reality, not your past one.

Adjustments tied to life events are strategic, not emotional. They keep the system aligned with your actual needs and goals.

Avoiding Over-Tinkering

Over-tinkering is the enemy of long-term success.

Making small changes constantly feels productive. It creates the illusion of control. In reality, it often increases trading costs, tax consequences, and behavioral mistakes.

In soccer, too many adjustments confuse players. Roles blur. Communication breaks down. Confidence drops. Execution suffers.

Investing is the same. A system only works if it is allowed to work.

Rebalancing is a tool, not a habit. It should be deliberate, infrequent, and purposeful. If you feel the urge to adjust because of headlines, fear, excitement, or boredom, that is a warning sign.

Real adjustments are driven by drift or meaningful life change, not noise.

Coach's Perspective: What Would Your Coach Say?

Your coach would slow things down.

They would say:

Stick to the plan.

Make smart adjustments.

Do not panic.

Trust the preparation.

Execute better.

Financially, that means reviewing calmly, adjusting intentionally, and avoiding unnecessary changes. The goal is clarity, not constant motion.

Coaches know that clarity wins matches, not chaos.

Game Situations and Decision Points

Situation one. One part of your portfolio is outperforming significantly.

Do you let it run unchecked because it feels good, or rebalance to maintain shape?

Situation two. Markets drop and fear rises.

Do you abandon the plan or rely on structure and discipline?

Situation three. Your life changes in a meaningful way.

Do you update the system or pretend nothing is different?

Each moment tests discipline and judgment more than knowledge.

Common Athlete Mistakes and Financial Parallels

Athletes overreact to bad halves. Investors overreact to short-term performance.

Athletes tinker constantly. Investors trade too often.

Athletes ignore fatigue and context. Investors ignore life changes.

Athletes chase momentum. Investors chase returns.

Recognizing these patterns keeps you grounded when pressure builds.

Winning the Long Game

Rebalancing is not about perfection. It is about staying aligned.

It keeps risk appropriate. It enforces discipline. It prevents small drifts from becoming big problems. It helps ensure your portfolio still matches your goals, not just market movements.

The best investors look boring from the outside. They make few changes. They stick to the plan. They adjust when it actually matters.

Just like great teams at halftime.

When you manage calmly and intentionally, the second half often takes care of itself.

Athlete Takeaways

Review investments on a schedule, not emotionally.

Rebalancing restores shape, not prediction.

Life changes matter more than market noise.

Over-tinkering creates mistakes. Discipline creates results.

Clarity beats panic, in matches and in markets.

Chapter 18: The Mental Side of Money

The hardest part of investing is not math. It is behavior.

Most athletes already understand this, even if they have never framed it this way. You can be in great shape, know the system, and still make bad decisions under pressure. Emotion changes execution. Noise changes focus. Confidence can turn into recklessness.

Money exposes the same weaknesses.

This chapter is about understanding the mental game behind financial decisions and building habits that keep emotion from hijacking the plan.

Fear, Greed, and Overconfidence

Fear, greed, and overconfidence are always present. They just show up at different times.

Fear appears during downturns. Prices fall. Headlines turn negative. Uncertainty grows. Fear whispers that doing something right now will make the discomfort stop. Selling feels like relief. Waiting feels risky. But decisions made to escape emotion often create long-term damage.

Greed shows up during rallies. Everyone seems to be making money. Opportunities feel endless. Greed convinces you that normal rules no longer apply. Risk feels smaller than it actually is. You stretch beyond your plan because it feels like "this is different."

Overconfidence sits quietly in the background. A few good outcomes create the belief that success came from skill alone. This leads to bigger bets, less diversification, and ignored warnings. Confidence is useful.

Overconfidence is expensive.

None of these emotions are flaws. They are human. The problem is acting on them without a system.

Great athletes do not eliminate emotion. They manage it. They feel pressure and still execute the right play.

Crowd Noise and Herd Behavior

Crowd noise matters.

In a stadium, noise can lift you or rattle you. Players who stay composed execute better. Players who get caught up in the crowd lose discipline and shape.

Markets have their own crowd noise. News cycles. Social media. Friends. Influencers. Confident opinions everywhere, often based on short-term movements.

Herd behavior feels safe because you are not alone. If everyone is doing it, it must be right. That logic has destroyed more wealth than almost any other mistake.

When markets rise, the herd piles in late, after much of the gain has already happened. When markets fall, the herd rushes out together, locking in losses. Both moves feel justified in the moment because they are popular.

Athletes understand this dynamic. Teams that chase momentum instead of structure get exposed quickly. They react instead of execute.

Independent thinking is uncomfortable. It requires trusting preparation over popularity.

Building Systems for Discipline

Discipline does not come from willpower. It comes from systems.

Athletes do not rely on motivation to train. Training is scheduled. Nutrition is planned. Recovery is built in. Systems remove decision fatigue and reduce the chance of skipping fundamentals.

Financial discipline works the same way.

Automated contributions ensure money is invested regularly without needing a new decision each month. Predefined allocation sets risk levels in advance. Scheduled reviews create structure. Rebalancing rules guide adjustments.

A good system makes the right action the default action.

When money moves automatically, fear has less opportunity to interfere. When rules are defined in advance, greed has fewer openings. When reviews are scheduled, overconfidence gets checked.

The goal is not to make decisions constantly. It is to make fewer, better decisions.

Staying Composed During Volatility

Volatility is where the mental game is tested most.

Markets move up and down. This is normal. The problem is how people respond.

Checking accounts too often increases anxiety. Reacting to daily swings creates stress. Interpreting every move as meaningful drains confidence and focus.

Composure comes from perspective.

Short-term volatility does not change long-term plans. Temporary declines do not equal permanent damage unless you act on them. Selling at the wrong time turns discomfort into loss.

Athletes know this lesson from competition. One mistake does not define a match. One bad half does not end a season. Panic does.

Staying composed means trusting preparation, not predictions. It means focusing on controllables like saving, allocation, and behavior, not outcomes you cannot control.

Coach's Perspective: What Would Your Coach Say?

Your coach would recognize emotional drift immediately.

They would say:

Stay locked in.

Next play.

Control what you can control.

Do not flinch.

Trust the work.

Financially, that means sticking to the plan when emotions spike. Not changing strategy because of noise. Executing fundamentals when pressure rises.

Coaches know that mental mistakes compound faster than physical ones.

Game Situations and Decision Points

Situation one. Markets fall sharply and fear is everywhere.

Do you sell to feel better right now, or stay disciplined according to your plan?

Situation two. A hot trend dominates conversation and social feeds.

Do you chase it because everyone else is, or stick to your strategy?

Situation three. Your portfolio performs well for a period of time.

Do you increase risk out of confidence, or maintain balance and discipline?

Each moment tests emotional control more than intelligence.

Common Athlete Mistakes and Financial Parallels

Athletes play too fast when rattled. Investors trade too often when nervous.

Athletes chase crowd energy. Investors follow the herd.

Athletes confuse confidence with invincibility. Investors overextend after wins.

Athletes abandon fundamentals under pressure. Investors abandon plans during volatility.

Recognizing these patterns gives you an edge. Awareness reduces mistakes.

Winning the Long Game

The mental side of money determines outcomes more than strategy.

You can have a solid plan and still fail if behavior breaks down. You can have a simple plan and succeed if discipline holds.

Markets will test patience. They will test confidence. They will test composure. There will always be reasons to feel urgency.

Your job is not to eliminate emotion. It is to build systems that keep emotion from making decisions for you.

That is how great athletes perform under pressure. That is how long-term financial success is built.

Athlete Takeaways

Fear, greed, and overconfidence never disappear. Manage them.

Crowd noise leads to herd mistakes. Trust preparation instead.

Systems create discipline when emotions rise.

Composure during volatility separates winners from regrets.

The mental game of money is the real competition.

Part V: The Full Season and the Long Career

S*occer careers are short. Financial lives are long.*

Soccer teaches urgency.

You train knowing the window is limited. Injuries happen. Roles change. Careers end sooner than expected. Every season matters because there may not be many of them.

Money operates on the opposite timeline.

Financial lives stretch decades beyond the final whistle. Decisions made early echo much longer than most athletes expect. The challenge is learning to think beyond the next match and plan for a full season, and then a long career after that.

This section is about zooming out.

Up to this point, the focus has been on fundamentals, protection, investing, and management. Now the conversation shifts to longevity. Taxes. Retirement. Housing. Career transitions. Family responsibilities. Legacy.

These topics rarely feel urgent until they are unavoidable. That delay is costly.

Great teams manage the entire season, not just individual matches. They plan rotations. They manage minutes. They protect players so performance holds up over time.

Financial planning works the same way.

Short-term decisions feel loud. Long-term consequences arrive quietly. This section helps you connect daily choices to outcomes years down the road.

It also acknowledges reality. Careers are unpredictable. Income is uneven. Life changes direction. Planning does not eliminate uncertainty, but it gives you options when circumstances shift.

Athletes often struggle here because the scoreboard disappears. There is no crowd. No film session. No coach enforcing accountability. Discipline becomes optional, which is exactly when it matters most.

This part of the book is about creating your own structure.

Financial success over a long career is not about perfection. It is about sustainability. Protecting what you build. Adjusting as life changes. Making sure the years after soccer are defined by choice, not regret.

The skills that helped you compete still apply. Patience. Preparation. Discipline. Vision.

This section shows how to use them when the season no longer has a clear end date.

Chapter 19: Taxes and Where You Hold the Ball

In soccer, possession is not just about keeping the ball. It is about where you keep it.

Holding the ball in the wrong area of the field invites pressure. Holding it in the right space gives you time, angles, and options. Two players can make the same pass, but the outcome changes entirely based on positioning.

Taxes work the same way.

Many athletes focus on what they invest in and ignore where they hold it. That mistake quietly drains returns year after year. Smart tax planning is not about tricks or loopholes. It is about positioning.

This chapter is about understanding how different accounts are taxed, how growth is treated over time, and how small decisions about placement can compound into meaningful differences.

Taxable vs Tax-Advantaged Accounts

Not all accounts are treated equally.

Taxable accounts are flexible. You can invest, withdraw, and move money freely. The tradeoff is that taxes apply along the way. Interest, dividends, and realized gains are generally taxed in the year they occur.

Tax-advantaged accounts are built for long-term growth. Retirement accounts, education accounts, and similar structures provide tax benefits in exchange for rules. Limits on contributions. Penalties for early withdrawal. Restrictions on use.

Neither type is better in isolation. They serve different roles.

Taxable accounts provide liquidity and flexibility. Tax-advantaged accounts provide efficiency and compounding power.

Athletes often lean too heavily in one direction. Some avoid tax-advantaged accounts because they want access. Others lock everything away and lack flexibility.

Good positioning means having both and understanding why each exists.

Tax-Deferred vs Tax-Free Growth

The timing of taxes matters as much as the rate.

Tax-deferred growth means you postpone taxes until later. Contributions may reduce taxable income today, and growth compounds without annual taxation. Taxes are paid when money is withdrawn.

Tax-free growth means taxes are paid upfront, but qualified withdrawals are not taxed later. Growth belongs fully to you.

Both approaches can be powerful. The right choice depends on income level, career stage, and future expectations.

Athletes early in their careers may benefit from one approach. Athletes later in their careers may benefit from another. The mistake is assuming one is always better.

The key is understanding tradeoffs, not chasing labels.

Deferring taxes gives you more capital working now. Paying taxes upfront gives you certainty later. Neither is wrong. Context decides.

Asset Location Basics

Asset location is one of the most overlooked concepts in personal finance.

It refers to which investments you place in which accounts.

Some investments generate frequent taxable income. Others grow primarily through price appreciation. Placing them strategically can reduce taxes without changing the investments themselves.

This is positioning, not prediction.

For example, assets that produce regular income may be better suited to tax-advantaged accounts. Assets that grow slowly or generate fewer taxable events may fit better in taxable accounts.

Athletes often focus on asset allocation but ignore asset location. That is like choosing the right players but putting them in the wrong positions.

The result is unnecessary pressure and lost efficiency.

Asset location does not require complexity. It requires awareness.

Common Tax Mistakes

Many tax mistakes come from inattention, not bad intent.

One common mistake is ignoring taxes entirely until April. Taxes are a year-long game, not a single deadline.

Another is making investment decisions based solely on tax fear. Avoiding growth to avoid taxes often costs more than the tax itself.

Some athletes sell investments without understanding the tax impact. Others trade too frequently, creating unnecessary taxable events.

Another mistake is assuming future tax situations will look exactly like today. Careers change. Income changes. Laws change. Planning requires flexibility.

Taxes punish reaction and reward preparation.

Coach's Perspective: What Would Your Coach Say?

Your coach would emphasize awareness and positioning.

They would say:

Know where you are on the field.

Protect possession.

Play smart, not rushed.

Use the space you have.

Think two plays ahead.

Financially, that means understanding account rules, planning ahead, and making decisions that support long-term efficiency instead of short-term convenience.

Great teams control space. Great investors control taxes.

Game Situations and Decision Points

Situation one. You invest in the same assets everywhere. Do you consider tax impact, or ignore positioning?

Situation two. You need liquidity. Do you pull from the most tax-efficient source or the most convenient one?

Situation three. Income spikes unexpectedly. Do you adjust strategy or repeat last year's approach?

Each decision affects how much of your return you actually keep.

Common Athlete Mistakes and Financial Parallels

Athletes hold the ball too long in dangerous areas. Investors hold assets in inefficient accounts.

Athletes play the right pass at the wrong time. Investors choose good investments in the wrong location.

Athletes focus only on attack. Investors focus only on returns and ignore taxes.

Athletes underestimate fatigue. Investors underestimate the drag of ongoing taxes.

Recognizing these patterns changes outcomes.

Winning the Long Game

Taxes are not a one-time obstacle. They are a permanent part of the match.

You do not win by avoiding them entirely. You win by positioning intelligently.

Small improvements in tax efficiency compound over time. Less leakage means more capital stays in play. More capital compounds. More options appear later.

When you understand where to hold the ball, you stop giving away possession unnecessarily.

That control shows up quietly, year after year.

Athlete Takeaways

- Taxes depend on where you hold the ball, not just what you own.
- Taxable and tax-advantaged accounts serve different roles.
- Asset location improves efficiency without changing strategy.
- Smart positioning keeps more of your return in play.

Chapter 20: Retirement Accounts and Financial Independence

Retirement sounds distant to most athletes.

It feels like something older people worry about. Something that comes later. Something you will deal with once life settles down.

That mindset is understandable. It is also costly.

Financial independence is not an age. It is a position. It is the point where your money can support your life without relying entirely on your next paycheck. Retirement accounts are the primary tools that help you reach that position.

This chapter explains how those tools work, why they matter, and how to use them intentionally across a long financial career.

Employer Plans and Pensions

Employer-sponsored plans are often the first exposure athletes have to investing.

These include workplace retirement plans that allow you to contribute directly from your paycheck. Many employers also offer matching contributions. That match is not a perk. It is compensation you earn by participating.

Failing to capture a match is like leaving guaranteed playing time unused.

Employer plans are powerful because they automate discipline. Contributions happen before money ever hits your checking account. You do not have to decide each month. The system handles it. Over time, this creates consistency that most people struggle to maintain on their own.

Some careers also include pensions. Pensions promise future income based on years of service and earnings. They can provide meaningful stability, but they are less common today and often misunderstood.

If you have access to a pension, understand how it works. Vesting schedules determine when you fully own the benefit. Benefit calculations determine how income is measured. Survivor options affect what happens to loved ones.

Employer plans and pensions form the backbone of retirement preparation. They are not exciting, but they are foundational.

Traditional and Roth IRAs

Individual retirement accounts give you control beyond your employer.

Traditional IRAs generally provide tax benefits upfront. Contributions may reduce taxable income today. Growth compounds without annual taxes. Withdrawals later are taxed as income.

Roth IRAs work in reverse. Contributions are made with after-tax money. Growth and qualified withdrawals are tax-free later.

Both are powerful. Neither is universally better.

The decision depends on income level, career stage, and expectations about the future. Early in a career, when income may be lower, paying taxes now through Roth contributions can make sense. Later, when income is higher, deferring taxes through traditional contributions may be more efficient.

Athletes often want a clear answer. There is not one.

The real advantage comes from having options. Diversifying tax treatment gives flexibility later. It allows you to manage income strategically in retirement instead of being locked into one tax situation.

Contribution and Withdrawal Rules

Retirement accounts reward patience and punish impatience.

Contribution limits exist to encourage steady, long-term saving rather than sudden large deposits. Staying within those rules keeps tax advantages intact.

Withdrawal rules are just as important.

Taking money out too early often triggers penalties and taxes. These rules exist to protect the long-term purpose of the account, which is future independence, not current spending.

This does not mean retirement accounts are untouchable forever. It means they are designed for a specific role in your overall system.

Athletes sometimes avoid retirement accounts because they fear losing access. The better approach is balance. Use retirement accounts for long-term growth. Use other accounts for flexibility and shorter-term goals.

Knowing the rules removes fear. Ignoring them creates mistakes.

Retirement Income Basics

Retirement is not about stopping work. It is about controlling choices.

Income in retirement often comes from multiple sources. Retirement accounts. Pensions. Personal savings. Investments. Sometimes part-time work, consulting, or business income.

The key is coordination.

You want income to be reliable. Taxes to be manageable. Risk to be appropriate for your stage of life. You want to draw money in a way that supports sustainability rather than short-term comfort.

Withdrawal strategies matter. Taking too much too early increases the chance of running out. Taking too little may unnecessarily limit lifestyle and enjoyment.

This is not about guessing. It is about planning.

Athletes are used to structured income while playing. Retirement requires building that structure intentionally, turning accumulated assets into reliable support.

The goal is not luxury. It is sustainability and freedom of choice.

Coach's Perspective: What Would Your Coach Say?

Your coach would emphasize preparation.

They would say:

Think ahead.

Do the work early.

Stack good days.

Do not wait until it is urgent.

Finish strong.

Financially, that means using retirement accounts consistently, understanding the rules, and building independence over time. Early preparation creates options. Late preparation limits them.

Coaches know that you cannot cram a season's worth of work into the last week.

Game Situations and Decision Points

Situation one. You change jobs.

Do you ignore old retirement accounts, or consolidate and understand what you have?

Situation two. Your income increases.

Do you raise lifestyle, contributions, or both? Growth in income is an opportunity to strengthen your future position.

Situation three. You consider early withdrawals.

Do you understand the long-term cost in lost growth, taxes, and penalties?

Each decision affects future freedom more than current comfort.

Common Athlete Mistakes and Financial Parallels

Athletes assume retirement is far away. Time moves faster than expected.

Athletes rely on future income. Careers are unpredictable, and injuries or changes can shift plans quickly.

Athletes avoid boring preparation. Retirement rewards boring consistency.

Athletes delay decisions. Financial independence favors early action, even in small amounts.

Recognizing these patterns prevents regret later.

Winning the Long Game

Retirement accounts are not about stopping. They are about control.

They give you leverage over time. They reduce dependence on any single paycheck. They create options when careers change unexpectedly. They turn your past effort into future freedom.

Financial independence is built quietly. Contribution by contribution. Year by year. Season by season.

You do not need to max everything immediately. You need to start and stay consistent.

That is how long careers, and long lives, are supported.

Athlete Takeaways

Employer plans and matches are core tools. Use them fully.

Traditional and Roth accounts provide different tax advantages. Options matter.

Rules exist to protect long-term outcomes. Know them.

Financial independence comes from preparation, not perfect timing.

Small, consistent actions today build freedom tomorrow.

Chapter 21: Housing and Big Life Transfers

Big purchases change the match.

Housing, vehicles, and other major life decisions are not just financial transactions. They shape cash flow, flexibility, stress levels, and long-term options. Make the right move at the right time and life feels manageable. Make the wrong move, or make the right move at the wrong time, and everything tightens.

Athletes often struggle here because these decisions feel like milestones. Buying a home. Upgrading a car. Locking something in. Progress feels tangible. The danger is confusing permanence with stability.

This chapter is about making big life moves with intention, not emotion.

Renting vs Buying

Renting and buying solve different problems.

Renting provides flexibility.

You are paying for use, not ownership. There is no long-term commitment, no surprise repair bills, and no capital tied up in one place. This matters when income is uneven, careers are changing, or location is uncertain. Renting makes it easier to adjust quickly.

Buying provides control and potential stability.

You lock in housing costs with a fixed mortgage, build equity over time, and reduce exposure to rent increases. Ownership can make sense when you plan to stay put, your income is stable, and your savings are strong.

The mistake athletes make is assuming buying is always the next step, or that renting means failure.

Homeownership concentrates risk. A large portion of your net worth becomes tied to one asset, one location, and one set of ongoing costs. That is not wrong, but it must match your stage of life.

Renting is not throwing money away. Buying is not automatically investing. Both are tools. Timing determines whether they help or hurt.

Mortgages and Down Payments

Mortgages are long-term commitments disguised as monthly payments.

Low monthly payments can make large purchases feel affordable. The total cost often tells a different story. Interest stretches over decades. Maintenance, property taxes, and insurance add up quietly.

A home payment is not just principal and interest. It is repairs, upgrades, and the unexpected.

Down payments matter because they shape risk.

A larger down payment reduces borrowing, lowers monthly obligations, and increases flexibility. It gives you a cushion if home values fluctuate or life changes. A smaller down payment preserves cash today but increases leverage and vulnerability.

There is no perfect answer. The right choice depends on job stability, savings, and comfort with risk.

Athletes often underestimate how limiting a large fixed payment can feel when income changes. Contracts end. Roles change. Injuries happen. Mortgages are easiest to manage when life is predictable. They are hardest when it is not.

Understanding the commitment matters more than qualifying for it.

Cars, Leases, and Financing Traps

Cars are one of the fastest ways to damage cash flow.

They depreciate quickly. They are easy to finance. Payments feel manageable until stacked on top of housing, insurance, and lifestyle expenses.

Leases can look attractive because payments are lower and upgrades are frequent. The tradeoff is permanence. You are always paying and never building equity. It becomes a lifestyle habit, not a transportation solution.

Financing traps often hide in details. Long loan terms that stretch payments out. Low introductory payments that rise later. Rolling negative equity from an old vehicle into a new loan. These decisions feel small but lock in years of obligation.

Athletes are often targeted with aggressive financing because income looks strong on paper. The mistake is assuming future income will always cover today's decision.

Transportation should support your life, not strain it. A vehicle should serve a function, not create pressure.

Planning Major Purchases

Major purchases deserve planning, not impulse.

That does not mean delaying forever. It means understanding tradeoffs before committing.

Ask simple questions:

How does this affect monthly cash flow?

What flexibility do I lose?

What happens if income drops?

What am I giving up to afford this?

Does this decision increase stress or reduce it?

Big purchases stack. Housing plus cars plus lifestyle upgrades can quietly eliminate margin. Margin is what protects you when something unexpected happens.

Athletes are used to structured environments where costs are managed for them. After sports, that structure disappears. Planning replaces protection.

Spacing matters.

Just like in soccer, timing and positioning determine outcomes. Making multiple big commitments at once increases risk. Spacing decisions out preserves control and recovery time.

Coach's Perspective: What Would Your Coach Say?

Your coach would slow you down.

They would say:

Know the situation.

Do not overcommit.

Think long-term.

Protect flexibility.

Do not beat yourself.

Financially, that means choosing stability over status, margin over maxing out, and planning over impulse.

Great teams manage energy and resources across the season. They do not burn everything early chasing one moment.

Game Situations and Decision Points

Situation one. You feel pressure to buy because others are buying.

Do you evaluate fit for your life, or chase milestones?

Situation two. A low monthly payment makes a purchase feel safe.

Do you examine the full long-term commitment?

Situation three. Multiple big purchases line up at once.

Do you space them out or overload yourself?

Each decision affects future freedom and stress.

Common Athlete Mistakes and Financial Parallels

Athletes confuse permanence with progress. Money requires flexibility.

Athletes underestimate long-term fatigue. Fixed payments compound pressure month after month.

Athletes rely on future performance. Careers and income paths change faster than expected.

Athletes chase image. Financial stability is rarely flashy.

Recognizing these patterns protects momentum and keeps you from being forced into defensive decisions later.

Winning the Long Game

Housing and major purchases should support your life, not define it.

The right decisions create stability, reduce stress, and preserve options. The wrong ones force constant pressure and limit choices. Financial freedom shrinks when fixed commitments grow too large.

You do not need to rush. You need to align decisions with reality, not emotion.

When big life transfers are planned thoughtfully, they stop feeling heavy. They become part of a system that works for you instead of against you.

That is how you manage the full season, not just the opening matches.

Athlete Takeaways

Renting and buying are strategic choices, not milestones.

Mortgages shape flexibility more than monthly payments suggest.

Vehicles are convenience tools, not status assets.

Big purchases should reduce stress, not increase it.

Plan major decisions to protect cash flow and future options.

Chapter 22: Your Career Is Your Academy

When you were playing, development did not stop once you made the team.

You trained year-round. You watched film. You learned new systems. You adapted to coaches, roles, and competition. The academy never closed. Every season built on the last.

Your career after soccer works the same way.

Too many former athletes treat work as something static. Get a job. Do the role. Collect a paycheck. That mindset limits growth and income far more than people realize. Your career is not a destination. It is a training environment.

This chapter is about learning how to see your career the way you once saw your development as a player.

Salary vs Total Compensation

Most people focus only on salary.

That is understandable. Salary is visible. It hits the bank account. It feels like the scoreline.

But salary is only part of compensation.

Benefits often make up a significant portion of what you are actually earning. Retirement contributions. Health insurance. Bonuses. Equity. Time off. Education support. Flexibility. These elements matter more than many athletes realize.

Two jobs with the same salary can have very different total value.

Ignoring benefits is like evaluating a player only on goals scored and ignoring defense, positioning, and work rate. You miss the full picture.

Understanding total compensation helps you make better decisions, especially when comparing roles or considering a move. Sometimes a slightly lower salary with better benefits leads to stronger long-term outcomes.

Job Changes and Benefits

Athletes are used to movement.

Teams change. Coaches change. Roles change. Transitions are normal. Careers after sports often involve multiple job changes as well.

Each transition is an opportunity, but also a risk.

When you change jobs, benefits reset. Waiting periods. Vesting schedules. Insurance coverage. Retirement plans. These details matter.

Many people focus only on the new role and forget to manage the transition itself. Old retirement accounts get ignored. Insurance gaps appear. Benefits are misunderstood.

Career moves should be evaluated as full transfers, not just new jerseys.

Before changing roles, understand what you are leaving behind and what you are gaining. Timing matters. Missing a match or vesting date can cost real money.

Smart transitions preserve momentum instead of resetting progress.

Negotiation Basics

Negotiation makes many athletes uncomfortable because it feels personal.

In reality, negotiation is positional, not emotional.

You negotiated playing time, roles, and expectations as an athlete, even if it was informal. Career negotiation works the same way. Preparation matters more than personality.

Know your value. Understand the market. Be clear about priorities. Compensation, flexibility, growth, stability. Not everything is about money.

Negotiation is not about winning a standoff. It is about aligning expectations.

Many people accept initial offers without discussion because they fear conflict. That hesitation compounds over time. Small differences early can become large gaps later.

Confidence without arrogance. Clarity without hostility. Preparation without entitlement. Those are the traits that work.

Side Income and Entrepreneurship

Athletes often have an edge when it comes to side income.

Discipline. Work ethic. Comfort with risk. Competitive drive. These traits translate well to entrepreneurship and additional income streams.

Side income can provide flexibility, accelerate savings, and reduce dependence on a single employer. It can also create distraction and burnout if unmanaged.

Not every opportunity is worth pursuing.

Some side income scales well. Others demand constant attention for limited return. The key is alignment with your time, skills, and long-term goals.

Entrepreneurship is not required for success. It is a tool, not a mandate.

Used intentionally, side income builds leverage. Used impulsively, it drains focus.

Coach's Perspective: What Would Your Coach Say?

Your coach would not let development stagnate.

They would say:

Keep improving.

Know your role.

Earn your opportunities.

Prepare for the next level.

Do not waste reps.

Financially, that means treating your career like training. Learning continuously. Making intentional moves. Understanding that income growth is built, not granted.

Coaches know that complacency kills progress faster than failure.

Game Situations and Decision Points

Situation one. A job offers higher salary but weaker benefits. Do you evaluate total compensation or chase the headline number?

Situation two. A new opportunity arises. Do you manage the transition carefully or rush the move?

Situation three. A side income idea excites you. Do you assess sustainability or act on impulse?

Each decision shapes long-term earning power.

Common Athlete Mistakes and Financial Parallels

Athletes assume performance alone drives opportunity. Careers reward strategy and positioning too.

Athletes focus on today's role. Careers require thinking multiple seasons ahead.

Athletes avoid negotiation. Income gaps widen silently.

Athletes overtrain without recovery. Side income without balance burns out quickly.

Recognizing these patterns protects growth.

Winning the Long Game

Your career is your academy.

Every role teaches something. Every transition builds experience. Every negotiation shapes future leverage.

Income growth is not about one big contract. It is about stacking skills, understanding value, and staying adaptable as the environment changes.

The most successful former athletes treat work the way they treated training. Intentional. Disciplined. Long-term.

When you see your career as development instead of destination, opportunities multiply.

That is how financial stability is built long after the uniform comes off.

Athlete Takeaways

- Salary is only part of compensation. Know the full package.
- Job changes should preserve momentum, not reset progress.
- Negotiation is preparation, not confrontation.
- Side income works best when aligned with long-term goals.

Chapter 23: Estate Planning Basics Everyone Needs

Estate planning sounds heavier than it is.

Most people picture massive estates, complex trusts, and end-of-life conversations they would rather avoid. That misunderstanding causes many athletes to delay planning far too long. Estate planning is not about how much you have. It is about control, clarity, and protecting the people you care about.

In soccer terms, this is about organizing the back line so confusion does not create unnecessary damage.

Estate planning is not optional once life gets more complex. It is a basic responsibility that prevents chaos when decisions cannot be made in real time.

Wills and Trusts

A will is the foundation.

It outlines who receives your assets, who is responsible for carrying out your wishes, and who cares for minor children if something happens. It names the person in charge of handling your affairs. Without a will, the state decides these things based on default rules. That process is slow, public, and rarely aligned with personal intent.

A will does not avoid court involvement, but it provides direction. It reduces uncertainty and conflict because your wishes are clearly documented.

Trusts add another layer.

Trusts can help manage assets during life, control how assets are distributed, protect privacy, and reduce administrative complexity. They are especially useful when there are children, blended families, special needs beneficiaries, or meaningful assets involved.

Trusts are not about status. They are about structure and control. They can allow assets to be distributed over time rather than all at once. They can help protect younger beneficiaries from receiving large sums too early.

Not everyone needs a complex trust. Everyone needs clarity. The right tool depends on situation, not net worth.

Beneficiaries and Account Titling

Many assets do not follow your will.

Retirement accounts, insurance policies, and certain bank and investment accounts pass according to beneficiary designations. If those are outdated or incorrect, your intentions do not matter. The form controls.

This is one of the most common and costly mistakes athletes make.

Life changes. Marriage. Divorce. Children. Career shifts. Beneficiaries must be reviewed regularly. A document signed years ago may no longer reflect your life.

Account titling matters as well. How an account is owned determines who controls it and what happens if someone dies or becomes incapacitated. Joint ownership, individual ownership, and trust ownership all have different outcomes.

Ignoring titling and beneficiaries is like assuming teammates know their roles without reviewing the lineup. Confusion leads to breakdowns at the worst time.

Simple reviews prevent major problems.

Powers of Attorney

Estate planning is not only about death.

Powers of attorney allow someone you trust to make financial or legal decisions if you cannot. Injury, illness, or incapacity can happen at any age. Athletes understand how quickly availability can change.

Without these documents, even close family members may be unable to act on your behalf without court involvement. That delay creates stress and logistical problems at the worst possible time.

Bills may go unpaid. Accounts may be frozen. Decisions may stall.

Powers of attorney are about continuity. They ensure that someone has the authority to step in so life keeps moving.

Athletes understand this concept well. When one player cannot perform their role, someone else needs clear authority to step in.

Healthcare Directives

Healthcare decisions are deeply personal.

Healthcare directives communicate your wishes if you cannot speak for yourself. They outline preferences for care and name someone to make medical decisions on your behalf.

These documents are not about expecting the worst. They are about removing uncertainty and conflict during stressful moments. Family members should not have to guess what you would want or argue under pressure.

Clear direction protects loved ones emotionally. It gives them confidence that they are following your wishes, not making impossible choices alone.

This is preparation, not pessimism.

Coach's Perspective: What Would Your Coach Say?

Your coach would demand organization and responsibility.

They would say:

Handle your business.

Protect your family.

Do not leave loose ends.

Be prepared before it matters.

Do the simple things right.

Financially, that means having documents in place, keeping them updated, and communicating intentions clearly. Estate planning is not about complexity. It is about avoiding self-inflicted mistakes.

Great teams avoid preventable errors.

Game Situations and Decision Points

Situation one. You assume everything goes to family automatically.

Have you confirmed that through documents and beneficiary designations?

Situation two. Life changes but documents stay the same.

Do you update them, or ignore the shift?

Situation three. A crisis happens without authority in place.

Who can act? How quickly? With what limitations?

Each decision affects how smoothly things are handled when pressure is highest.

Common Athlete Mistakes and Financial Parallels

Athletes delay boring preparation. Estate issues punish delay.

Athletes assume intentions are obvious. Legal systems require documentation.

Athletes focus on performance, not structure. Estate planning is structure.

Athletes avoid uncomfortable conversations. Avoidance creates confusion later.

Recognizing these patterns prevents unnecessary hardship for the people you care about most.

Winning the Long Game

Estate planning is not about predicting the future. It is about preparing for it.

It protects loved ones. It preserves privacy. It reduces stress and conflict. It ensures your wishes are followed instead of guessed.

You do not need perfection. You need completion and updates over time.

When estate planning basics are handled, everything else feels lighter. Decisions are clearer. Families are protected. You remove uncertainty before it becomes a crisis.

That is quiet leadership.

Athlete Takeaways

Wills and trusts create clarity and control.

Beneficiaries and account titling override assumptions. Review them regularly.

Powers of attorney protect continuity during incapacity.

Healthcare directives remove uncertainty when it matters most.

Estate planning is responsibility, not complexity.

Chapter 24: Talking About Money With Family

Money conversations inside families are rarely about math. They are about expectations, roles, fear, pride, and responsibility. That is why so many families avoid them until something breaks. When the conversation finally happens, it is rushed, emotional, and reactive.

Athletes understand this dynamic. Teams that communicate early avoid chaos late. Teams that avoid hard conversations pay for it under pressure.

Talking about money with family is not about control. It is about clarity.

This chapter focuses on building understanding across generations while setting healthy expectations and boundaries that protect relationships as much as finances.

Teaching Kids About Money

Kids learn money the same way they learn the game.

They watch. They copy. They absorb habits long before they understand rules. How you talk about money, how you spend, how you handle stress around bills, all of it becomes their baseline.

If money is never discussed, kids do not become neutral. They become confused. They fill the gaps with assumptions, anxiety, or misinformation picked up from friends or media.

Teaching kids about money does not require complex systems or perfect execution. It requires consistency.

Simple concepts matter most. Money is earned. Some is saved. Some is spent intentionally. Some is given. Waiting is normal. Tradeoffs exist.

Let them see decisions. Explain choices in age-appropriate ways. Involve them in small financial responsibilities as they grow.

The goal is not to raise financial experts. It is to raise kids who are comfortable making decisions, asking questions, and learning from mistakes.

Athletes know this from development. Fundamentals come before tactics. Reps matter more than lectures.

Money should feel like a tool, not a source of fear or secrecy.

College and Young Adults

College and early adulthood are where money mistakes become real.

Credit cards, student loans, rent, taxes, and income arrive all at once. Structure disappears. Freedom increases. Consequences become personal.

Parents often struggle with where to draw the line.

Too much control delays maturity. Too little guidance leaves young adults exposed to avoidable mistakes.

The right role is coach, not manager.

Talk about credit honestly. Explain interest and how debt grows. Discuss budgeting in real numbers, not just concepts. Share how mistakes compound over time, but also that mistakes can be recovered from with good habits.

Let young adults make decisions, but do not leave them uninformed.

Athletes recognize this balance. You do not step onto the field for someone else. You prepare them to compete on their own. You give feedback, not control.

The goal is confidence, not dependence.

Aging Parents and Caregiving

Later in life, roles often reverse.

Parents who once provided guidance may need help managing complexity. Health changes. Cognitive decline. Caregiving needs increase. Financial decisions become more urgent and more sensitive.

Avoiding these conversations does not protect anyone. It delays preparation and increases stress during crisis.

Key topics include organization, access, and expectations. Where accounts are held. Who can help if needed. How care will be funded. What wishes exist for living arrangements and medical decisions.

These conversations require respect and patience. Pride and independence are real factors.

This is not about taking control. It is about reducing uncertainty and protecting dignity.

Athletes understand leadership here. Tough conversations protect the team. Silence creates vulnerability.

Family Expectations and Boundaries

This is where many money conversations break down.

Family expectations are often unspoken. Assumptions replace agreements. Boundaries blur.

Who helps whom. How much support is expected. What is temporary versus ongoing. What conditions apply. These questions matter more than people realize.

Without boundaries, resentment grows quietly. Financial stress mixes with emotional stress.

Setting boundaries is not selfish. It is protective.

Boundaries clarify what you can do, what you cannot do, and under what conditions help exists. They protect relationships by removing ambiguity and preventing misunderstandings.

Athletes know this lesson. Roles must be clear. When responsibilities overlap without clarity, performance suffers. Teams work best when everyone understands their lane.

Financial boundaries allow generosity without obligation and support without sacrificing your own stability.

Coach's Perspective: What Would Your Coach Say?

Your coach would demand communication and accountability.

They would say:

Talk early.

Be clear.

Set expectations.

Protect the team.

Handle it before it becomes urgent.

Financially, that means having ongoing conversations, not one-time confrontations. Clarifying roles before stress forces decisions.

Great teams communicate constantly, not just when something goes wrong.

Game Situations and Decision Points

Situation one. You avoid money talks to keep peace.

Does silence actually reduce tension, or does it allow confusion to build?

Situation two. A family member needs help.

Do you clarify expectations, timeline, and boundaries, or create open-ended obligation?

Situation three. Aging parents resist planning.

Do you wait until a crisis, or lead respectfully and patiently now?

Each choice shapes long-term family dynamics and emotional health.

Common Athlete Mistakes and Financial Parallels

Athletes avoid uncomfortable conversations. Teams break down under pressure.

Athletes overextend themselves trying to do everything. Burnout follows.

Athletes assume alignment without checking. Money requires explicit clarity.

Athletes delay leadership. Problems grow quietly until they are harder to fix.

Recognizing these patterns prevents conflict and regret.

Winning the Long Game

Money conversations are not single events.

They evolve as families grow, roles change, and responsibilities shift. Avoiding them does not preserve harmony. It postpones tension and makes future conversations harder.

Handled well, these conversations build trust. They reduce anxiety. They protect relationships. They create shared understanding instead of silent pressure.

Families that communicate early handle change better. Families that wait react poorly when pressure arrives.

Leadership at home matters as much as leadership on the field.

Athlete Takeaways

Kids learn money habits through example and repetition.

Young adults need coaching, not control.

Aging parents require preparation handled with respect.

Clear expectations and boundaries protect relationships and finances.

Communication is leadership, in families and on teams.

Part VI: Playing the Long Game

Every athlete understands the difference between winning a moment and winning a career.

Moments are loud. Highlights get attention. Big plays feel decisive. But careers are built in quieter ways. Through consistency. Through discipline. Through decisions that do not make headlines but hold up over time.

Money rewards the same approach.

By this point in the book, you have covered fundamentals, protection, investing, management, and long-term planning. This final section zooms out and focuses on durability. How to protect what you build. How to avoid the traps that derail progress. How to make decisions that still work decades from now.

Playing the long game means accepting that perfection is impossible.

Markets change. Careers change. Life changes. The goal is not to predict every outcome. The goal is to stay flexible, disciplined, and prepared enough to adapt without panic.

Athletes often struggle here because the structure disappears. No coach sets the schedule. No season defines the timeline. Accountability becomes internal. That is exactly when systems matter most.

This section is about awareness.

Knowing when to ask for help. Recognizing bad advice and empty promises. Understanding that avoiding big mistakes matters more than chasing big wins. Accepting that consistency beats intensity.

Long-term success is not built through genius or luck. It is built through habits that survive stress, boredom, and change.

The best players know when to slow the game down. The best investors know when to do nothing.

This part of the book is about finishing strong and setting yourself up to keep winning long after the uniform comes off.

Chapter 25: Advisors, Scams, and Long-Term Success

Every long season exposes the truth.

Early on, talent can cover mistakes. Speed hides poor positioning. Energy masks weak fundamentals. A few lucky breaks make things look easier than they are.

Late in the game, that changes.

Fatigue sets in. Margins shrink. Pressure increases. Discipline decides outcomes. Shortcuts that worked for a moment eventually fail. What remains are habits, systems, and the people you trust.

Money works the same way.

This final chapter is about protecting what you build over decades. Knowing when to ask for help. Knowing who to trust. Knowing how to avoid traps that quietly derail progress. And knowing what actually drives long-term success once the excitement fades.

Because wealth is not built in highlight moments. It is built in the quiet middle when nobody is watching.

When to Seek Professional Help

Athletes are not trained to do everything alone.

You work with coaches, trainers, medical staff, and analysts because specialization matters. You focus on performance while others support the system around you. No serious athlete says, "I'll just rehab this injury myself" or "I'll design my own training science." You build a team.

Money deserves the same respect.

Professional help makes sense when complexity rises or mistakes become expensive. Career transitions. Large income swings. Taxes across multiple states. Business ownership. Investing across several accounts. Estate planning. Family changes. These moments create blind spots even for disciplined people.

Seeking help is not giving up control. It is adding perspective and accountability.

The right advisor does not replace your judgment. They sharpen it. They help you see tradeoffs, avoid blind spots, and stay aligned with your long-term plan when life gets busy. They slow you down when emotion rises and help you move when hesitation is costly.

Waiting too long often turns manageable decisions into damage control. Strong performers ask for coaching early. Struggling ones wait until options shrink.

That pattern holds in sports and money.

Types of Financial Advisors

Not all advisors play the same position.

Some focus primarily on investments. Some focus on comprehensive planning that includes taxes, insurance, and estate considerations. Some specialize in business planning, retirement income, or risk management. Some operate more like sales professionals than planners.

Titles alone do not tell you how someone is compensated or whose interests come first.

Understanding incentives matters.

Advisors paid by commissions may be rewarded for transactions or product sales. Advisors paid by fees may be rewarded for long-term relationships and asset growth. Neither model is automatically good or bad. Transparency is what matters most.

A quality advisor explains how they are paid, what services they provide, and what they do not do. They ask questions before making recommendations. They educate instead of rushing. They are comfortable when you ask for clarification and they welcome a second opinion.

The right advisor helps you stay disciplined, avoid major mistakes, and build systems that work even when your attention is elsewhere.

You are not hiring someone to impress you. You are hiring someone to protect your blind side.

Recognizing Scams and Bad Advice

Athletes are frequent targets.

Visibility, income potential, and trust in relationships attract bad actors. Scams often sound convincing because they are designed to bypass logic and trigger emotion.

Common warning signs appear repeatedly. Urgency. Exclusivity. Guaranteed results. Pressure to act now. Resistance to questions. Claims that others "would not understand" or "this opportunity will disappear."

If something cannot withstand simple scrutiny, it does not deserve your money.

Bad advice is not always illegal. It is often overconfident, oversimplified, or disconnected from your actual situation. Advice that ignores taxes, liquidity needs, risk tolerance, or downside scenarios is incomplete.

Confidence is not competence. Transparency is.

Slow down when someone speeds you up. Ask questions when someone discourages them. Real opportunities survive careful review.

Ten Common Financial Mistakes

Most people do not make one huge mistake. They make small ones repeatedly until the damage compounds.

- Waiting too long to start
- Chasing returns instead of building systems

- Taking risks you do not understand
- Ignoring taxes, fees, and friction
- Overconcentrating in one idea or asset
- Reacting emotionally to market swings
- Confusing income with long-term wealth
- Avoiding uncomfortable but necessary conversations
- Trusting hype over fundamentals
- Failing to adjust as life changes

Avoiding these errors matters more than finding perfect strategies. Defense wins long seasons.

Ten Rules for Long-Term Success

None of these rules are exciting. All of them work.

- Start early and stay consistent
- Control what you can control
- Build systems that remove emotion
- Diversify and respect risk
- Protect downside before chasing upside
- Understand where and how your money is held
- Review intentionally, not constantly
- Ask for help when complexity rises
- Keep money aligned with real life
- Think in decades, not moments

These are fundamentals, not tricks. Fundamentals age well.

Coach's Perspective: What Would Your Coach Say?

Your coach would focus on discipline and accountability.

They would say:

Trust the process.

Do the boring work.

Avoid shortcuts.

Stay consistent.

Finish strong.

Financially, that means choosing structure over excitement and habits over hype. The fundamentals win over time. The players who last are rarely the flashiest. They are the most disciplined.

Winning the Long Game

Long-term success is not about avoiding every mistake. It is about avoiding the big ones again and again. It is about building systems that catch small errors before they become large ones.

It is about staying patient when others panic. Staying disciplined when others chase. Staying grounded when noise gets loud.

The same traits that made you competitive still apply. Preparation. Accountability. Consistency. Perspective.

Money is just another arena where those traits decide outcomes.

When you play the long game, results compound quietly. Options expand. Stress shrinks. Freedom increases. You stop reacting and start choosing.

That is real winning.

Athlete Takeaways

Seek professional help before complexity becomes damage.

Transparency matters more than titles or confidence.

Urgency and guarantees are warning signs.

Avoid repeated small mistakes. They compound.

Discipline and consistency win over decades, not moments.

Chapter 26: Losing the Schedule and Rebuilding Structure

One of the hardest transitions after soccer has nothing to do with money.

It is the loss of the schedule.

When you are playing, life is structured for you. Training times. Meetings. Travel. Film. Recovery. Someone is always setting the calendar and holding you accountable. Discipline is enforced externally.

You do not have to decide every day whether you will train. It is already decided.

When that structure disappears, life feels freer at first. Then it gets harder.

This chapter is about understanding why that happens and how to rebuild structure intentionally so financial habits do not quietly fall apart.

From Mandatory Workouts to Optional Discipline

Mandatory workouts create consistency.

You show up because you have to. You train whether you feel like it or not. You follow a plan even when energy is low. Over time, results compound because discipline is non-negotiable. Structure does the heavy lifting.

After sports, discipline becomes optional.

No one tells you when to wake up. No one checks attendance. No one reviews effort. No one says, "We start at 8." The responsibility shifts entirely to you.

This change exposes a gap most athletes are not prepared for. Motivation fluctuates. Habits slip. Small decisions get postponed. Days feel less defined. Progress feels less visible.

Financial habits suffer the same way.

Saving becomes something you will do later. Budgeting feels unnecessary this month. Investing gets delayed because you are "figuring things out." You tell yourself you will organize everything when life settles down.

None of this feels dramatic in the moment. It just slowly erodes momentum.

Structure used to protect you from yourself. Without it, effort has to be intentional.

How Lack of Structure Quietly Breaks Financial Habits

Financial habits fail quietly.

You do not wake up one day broke. You drift there.

Without a schedule, actions become reactive instead of proactive. Bills get paid late because there was no routine. Accounts go unchecked because there was no review time. Spending fills gaps left by boredom, stress, or lack of direction. Investing feels distant because there is no defined "practice time" for it.

The danger is not bad intentions. It is inconsistency.

Athletes are used to training blocks and seasons. There are phases, goals, and check-ins. Money without structure feels abstract. There is no scoreboard. No game day to prepare for. No coach demanding progress.

Without deadlines, discipline fades.

Rebuilding structure is not about being rigid. It is about creating anchors that keep habits alive even when life feels unstructured.

Replacing Practice Schedules With Personal Systems

The solution is not motivation. It is systems.

Athletes already know this. Training works because it is scheduled, repeatable, and tracked. Financial habits need the same treatment.

Automate savings and investing so money moves before you can second-guess it. Set review dates on your calendar just like training sessions. Create routines for budgeting, planning, and checking accounts. Use reminders, tools, and checklists.

Structure turns discipline from a decision into a default.

Personal systems replace external enforcement. They create rhythm. They reduce friction. They protect progress when motivation dips, when life gets busy, or when distractions rise.

You do not need perfect systems. You need consistent ones.

A simple monthly money check-in done every month beats an elaborate system done twice a year.

Discipline Transfer: The Identity Shift

This transition is also about identity.

In sports, discipline was part of the environment. After sports, discipline becomes part of your personal identity. It is no longer something required of you. It is something you choose.

That shift can feel uncomfortable because it removes external pressure. But it also creates ownership.

You are not losing discipline. You are transferring it from the locker room to your own life.

The athletes who thrive after sports are not necessarily the most talented. They are the ones who learn to self-impose structure. They build routines that support health, career, and finances without being forced.

Money becomes another training category.

Coach's Perspective: What Would Your Coach Say?

Your coach would recognize the issue immediately.

They would say:

Discipline does not disappear. It transfers.

Handle your own schedule.

No excuses.

Do the work when no one is watching.

Consistency wins.

Financially, that means creating structure even when no one is enforcing it. Setting your own standards. Showing up for your future self.

Champions are built in empty gyms and quiet mornings. Financial stability is built the same way.

Game Situations and Decision Points

Situation one. No deadlines exist for financial tasks.

Do you drift, or design structure?

Situation two. Motivation drops.

Do habits disappear, or do systems hold?

Situation three. Life gets busy and unpredictable.

Do routines collapse, or adapt and continue?

Each choice shapes long-term outcomes more than any single investment decision.

Common Athlete Mistakes and Financial Parallels

Athletes rely on motivation. Systems outlast motivation.

Athletes wait for pressure to perform. Financial pressure arrives late, after habits have already slipped.

Athletes underestimate drift. Small lapses compound quietly.

Athletes confuse freedom with flexibility. True flexibility comes from structure, not absence of it.

Recognizing these patterns allows you to rebuild control before drift turns into damage.

Winning the Long Game

Structure is not restrictive. It is freeing.

It creates momentum. It removes decision fatigue. It keeps progress moving even when life gets messy, uncertain, or emotionally heavy.

The most successful former athletes rebuild structure on their own terms. They create systems that replace what sports once enforced. They protect their time, energy, and money with routines.

When structure returns, clarity improves. Confidence rises. Financial habits stabilize. Stress decreases because you know what is being handled and when.

You are not losing discipline. You are redefining it.

That is what long-term success looks like after the final whistle.

Athlete Takeaways

Losing the schedule removes external accountability.

Optional discipline breaks habits quietly.

Systems replace motivation and protect progress.

Structure creates freedom when designed intentionally.

Discipline after sports is a choice. Make it part of your identity.

Chapter 27: From Teammates to Coworkers

Leaving sports does not just change how you train. It changes how you relate to people.

For years, teammates were family. Roles were clear. Authority was obvious. Feedback was direct. Effort was visible. Everyone knew the goal and how success was measured.

Then you enter the workplace.

Suddenly, the rules feel unspoken. Expectations are vague. Feedback is indirect. Authority exists, but it does not look like coaching. Performance is harder to measure. Politics show up where preparation used to matter most.

This shift catches many former athletes off guard. Not because they lack ability, but because the environment is unfamiliar.

This chapter explains why the workplace can feel so foreign after sports and how that disconnect quietly affects income growth and career stability.

Why the Workplace Feels Foreign After Sports

In sports, alignment is built in.

Everyone is working toward the same outcome. Win the match. Win the season. Improve performance. Roles may differ, but purpose is shared.

Workplaces rarely operate that cleanly.

People have different incentives. Some want promotions. Some want stability. Some want visibility. Some want to avoid risk. The scoreboard is not obvious, and goals can change without warning.

Former athletes often assume effort will be noticed the same way it was in sports. That assumption creates frustration when results do not follow.

The environment is not worse. It is different.

Understanding that difference is the first step to adapting without losing momentum.

Authority Without Coaches

In sports, authority is clear.

Coaches decide lineups. They control playing time. They correct mistakes openly. You know who sets direction and how decisions get made.

In the workplace, authority is layered and indirect.

Your manager may not be a coach. They may not give frequent feedback. They may not advocate for you unless prompted. Decision-making often happens behind closed doors.

Former athletes wait for coaching that never comes.

Income growth suffers when you assume someone else is tracking your development. Promotions and raises often require visibility, communication, and self-advocacy.

This does not mean being arrogant or demanding. It means understanding that leadership and feedback are not automatic anymore.

You have to manage up as well as perform.

Feedback Without Film

Film made everything clear.

You could see mistakes. You could see progress. You could measure improvement. Feedback was concrete.

Workplace feedback is rarely that direct.

Performance reviews may be annual. Comments may be vague. Praise may be subtle. Criticism may be indirect or avoided entirely.

Former athletes struggle here because they are used to clarity.

Without feedback, it is easy to assume things are fine when they are not. Or to assume things are wrong when they are not.

Both scenarios stall growth.

Seeking feedback becomes a skill. Asking questions. Clarifying expectations. Requesting examples. Following up.

In the absence of film, you have to create your own feedback loops.

Politics, Ambiguity, and Unclear Expectations

This is where frustration peaks.

In sports, politics exist, but performance still matters. In the workplace, politics and perception can outweigh effort.

That feels unfair to former athletes who were taught that work speaks for itself.

Ambiguity shows up everywhere. What does success look like. Who decides. What matters most right now. What changes next quarter.

Unclear expectations create hesitation. Hesitation slows progress. Slow progress limits income growth.

This does not mean compromising integrity. It means understanding the environment.

Learning how decisions are made. Who influences outcomes. What gets rewarded. What gets ignored.

Ignoring politics does not make them disappear. It just makes you less prepared.

How This Impacts Income Growth and Career Stability

Income growth after sports is not linear.

Athletes often expect performance alone to drive opportunity. In the workplace, visibility, communication, and alignment matter just as much.

If expectations are unclear, you may excel at the wrong things. If feedback is missing, you may repeat mistakes unknowingly. If authority is indirect, you may wait too long for permission that never comes.

Career stability suffers when roles feel uncertain and progress feels unpredictable.

The solution is not cynicism. It is adaptation.

Former athletes who thrive learn to translate their discipline into this new environment. They clarify expectations early. They seek feedback intentionally. They communicate goals. They build relationships without losing authenticity.

They stop waiting for a coach to call them in.

Coach's Perspective: What Would Your Coach Say?

Your coach would recognize the adjustment immediately.

They would say:

Learn the system.

Know what wins here.

Ask for feedback.

Communicate clearly.

Control what you can control.

Financially, this translates into understanding how income growth actually happens in your field, not how you wish it worked.

Game Situations and Decision Points

Situation one. You work hard but receive little feedback. Do you assume all is well or ask for clarity?

Situation two. Promotions seem political. Do you disengage or learn how decisions are made?

Situation three. Expectations shift without notice. Do you react emotionally or recalibrate strategically?

Each response shapes career trajectory.

Common Athlete Mistakes and Financial Parallels

Athletes wait for coaching that never comes. Careers stall.

Athletes assume effort is visible. Income growth requires communication.

Athletes avoid politics. Politics still influence outcomes.

Athletes disengage when frustrated. Disengagement reduces stability.

Recognizing these patterns restores control.

Winning the Long Game

The workplace is not the locker room.

It does not reward effort the same way. It does not provide clarity automatically. It does not measure performance cleanly.

Former athletes who succeed learn the new game without abandoning their values.

They bring discipline, accountability, and preparation into an environment that requires additional skills. Communication. Self-advocacy. Perspective.

Once that adjustment is made, income growth becomes steadier and careers become more resilient.

You are not losing your edge.

You are learning a new system.

Athlete Takeaways

- The workplace operates on different rules than sports.
- Authority and feedback are indirect and must be sought.
- Ambiguity and politics affect income growth.
- Adapting the mindset restores stability and momentum.

Chapter 28: When No One Is Watching Anymore

One of the biggest shocks after sports is not physical. It is psychological.

For years, someone was always watching. Coaches. Teammates. Trainers. Fans. Film. Accountability was constant. Effort was visible. Mistakes were corrected quickly. Feedback loops were tight.

Then it stops.

No one is tracking reps. No one is checking attendance. No one is grading effort. Life gets quieter, and with that quiet comes risk.

This chapter is about what happens when accountability disappears and why so many former athletes struggle not because they lost discipline, but because discipline lost its structure.

The Discipline Gap After Accountability Disappears

In sports, discipline is enforced.

You train because you have to. You recover because it is scheduled. You prepare because performance depends on it. The environment is designed to make discipline the default.

After sports, discipline becomes optional.

No whistle. No roster spot on the line. No consequences this week for slipping. The gap shows up slowly. Skipped workouts. Delayed saving. Ignored planning. None of it feels dramatic. It just becomes normal.

Former athletes are not lazy. They are unaccustomed to self-generated accountability at this scale. Their discipline was real, but it was supported by systems, schedules, and social pressure.

When pressure disappears, habits drift.

Financial habits suffer the same way. Saving becomes something you will do later. Investing feels unnecessary right now. Planning gets postponed until life "settles down."

Without pressure, consistency fades.

Why Former Athletes Self-Sabotage Without Pressure

Self-sabotage rarely feels intentional.

It looks like comfort. Avoidance. Distraction. Justification. "I deserve a break." "I'll start next month." "It's not urgent."

Without a scoreboard or season, progress feels abstract. There is no immediate reward for discipline and no immediate penalty for neglect. The consequences of today's decisions are years away, which makes them easy to ignore.

Former athletes may chase short-term comfort because long-term goals feel distant. Money gets spent instead of saved. Time gets filled instead of invested. Easy choices replace intentional ones.

This is not a character flaw. It is a structural problem.

Athletes were built to respond to pressure, deadlines, and performance environments. Remove pressure without replacing structure and behavior changes.

Comfort vs Growth Decisions

In sports, comfort is dangerous.

Comfort means you are not pushing limits. Growth happens at the edge of discomfort, where effort stretches capacity. Coaches push you there on purpose.

After sports, comfort becomes seductive. Stable job. Predictable routine.

Minimal stress. Easy spending. None of these are bad on their own, but they can quietly stall progress.

Financially, comfort shows up as avoiding risk entirely or ignoring planning because things feel fine right now. "I'm doing okay" replaces "I'm building for the future."

Growth requires intentional discomfort. Budgeting when you would rather spend. Saving when you could upgrade. Learning when you feel tired. Saying no to short-term pleasure to protect long-term freedom.

Without a coach pushing you, you have to decide when to lean into growth.

That decision, repeated over time, determines long-term outcomes.

Translating "Grind Culture" Into Adult Life

Grind culture works in sports because it is structured.

Hard work is scheduled. Recovery is enforced. Purpose is clear. Progress is measured. Effort is directed toward defined goals.

In adult life, grind without structure leads to burnout.

Former athletes often try to replicate intensity without direction. Long hours. Overworking. Saying yes to everything. Hustling constantly without clarity.

This does not create progress. It creates exhaustion.

The goal is not grinding harder. It is working smarter.

Translate effort into systems. Automate habits. Set boundaries. Define goals. Measure progress. Build routines that protect energy instead of draining it.

Discipline without structure is just fatigue. Discipline with structure becomes momentum.

Why Money Mistakes Show Up Years Later

Money mistakes rarely show up immediately.

Skipping savings at 25 does not hurt at 26. It shows up at 35 when compounding time is gone. Ignoring investing early does not feel painful until you realize how much growth was missed. Overspending early feels manageable until fixed costs crowd out flexibility later.

Former athletes often say, "I wish I had known earlier."

The delay is the trap.

Without accountability, mistakes accumulate quietly. There is no film session to catch them. No coach to intervene. No teammate calling you out. Financial drift goes unnoticed until it becomes visible in stress, limited options, or regret.

By the time consequences appear, options feel tighter.

The solution is early structure, not late regret.

Coach's Perspective: What Would Your Coach Say?

Your coach would not tolerate drift.

They would say:

Do the work when no one is watching.

Comfort is the enemy.

Earn it every day.

Discipline equals freedom.

Stack good days.

Financially, that means showing up consistently even when results are not visible yet. Making the boring choices. Protecting habits. Acting before pressure forces you to.

Championships are built in empty gyms and quiet mornings. Financial stability is built the same way.

Game Situations and Decision Points

Situation one. No deadlines exist for financial tasks.

Do you drift or design discipline?

Situation two. Comfort feels good right now.

Do you choose ease or growth?

Situation three. Money decisions feel small.

Do you ignore them or act early knowing they compound?

Each choice compounds, just like training or skipping reps.

Common Athlete Mistakes and Financial Parallels

Athletes rely on pressure. Pressure disappears.

Athletes chase comfort. Growth stalls.

Athletes grind without structure. Burnout follows.

Athletes delay planning. Consequences arrive later, not immediately.

Recognizing these patterns restores control. Awareness creates the opportunity to rebuild structure intentionally.

Winning the Long Game

When no one is watching, habits matter most.

The former athletes who thrive build structure where sports once provided it. They create accountability systems. They choose growth intentionally. They turn discipline into identity instead of environment.

The work is quieter now. The stakes are higher.

Money does not care who is watching. It responds to consistency, not motivation.

When you master discipline without pressure, long-term success becomes possible. Not because life is easier, but because you built systems strong enough to carry you when motivation fades.

Athlete Takeaways

Accountability disappears. Discipline must be rebuilt.

Self-sabotage often looks like comfort.

Growth requires intentional discomfort.

Structure protects discipline when pressure is gone.

Early financial habits prevent late regret.

Chapter 29: Redefining Winning After the Uniform Comes Off

When you are an athlete, winning is clear.

The scoreboard tells you. The standings confirm it. Film backs it up. Success is visible, measurable, and shared. You know where you stand and what you are playing for. The goal is defined, and the path to improvement is structured.

When the uniform comes off, that clarity disappears.

No scoreboard. No rankings. No coach defining success. No season schedule. In that vacuum, many former athletes start chasing substitutes for winning without realizing it.

This chapter is about redefining what winning actually means after sports and building a new scoreboard that reflects real life, not borrowed standards.

Why Chasing Status Replaces Chasing Performance

In sports, performance earns status.

You play well, you earn respect. You contribute, you move up. Status is a byproduct of effort, preparation, and results.

After sports, status often replaces performance.

Without clear metrics, people reach for visible markers. Job titles. Income numbers. Houses. Cars. Social media signals. These become stand-ins for progress. They are easy to see and easy to compare.

The problem is not ambition. It is misalignment.

Status markers are visible. Performance in adult life is often invisible. Stability. Consistency. Emotional health. Financial discipline. These do not show up in highlight reels.

Former athletes are competitive by nature. Without a game to focus that energy, comparison fills the gap. You start measuring yourself against others' surface-level signals instead of your own deeper progress.

Chasing status feels like winning until it does not. It feels good temporarily, then pressure returns because there is always another level.

Income vs Fulfillment

Income matters. It provides security, freedom, and options. It reduces stress and creates flexibility.

But income alone does not equal success.

Many former athletes reach income goals and still feel off. Burned out. Disconnected. Unfulfilled. That confusion is jarring because money was supposed to mean winning.

Fulfillment comes from alignment. Work that fits your values. Time for relationships. Health. Growth. Contribution. Feeling that your effort means something beyond a paycheck.

Income supports fulfillment. It does not replace it.

Athletes are used to sacrifice because the purpose is clear. Early mornings, hard practices, recovery discipline all make sense because the goal is defined.

Adult life requires choosing what is worth sacrificing for.

That decision defines success more than income alone.

Titles, Houses, Cars, and Comparison Traps

Status symbols are powerful because they are visible.

A new title. A bigger house. A nicer car. They signal progress to others. They also create pressure to maintain an image. Expenses rise. Expectations rise. Freedom shrinks quietly.

Comparison accelerates quickly.

Someone always has more. Someone always looks ahead. Someone always appears to be winning on the surface. Chasing that ladder never ends.

Athletes understand this from competition. There is always another opponent. Another record. Another level. In sports, that pursuit is structured and time-bound. In life, it can become endless and exhausting.

The trap is confusing external validation with internal satisfaction.

Winning becomes about looking successful instead of feeling grounded. Decisions get driven by perception instead of alignment.

What "Success" Actually Looks Like in Your 30s and 40s

Success in your 30s and 40s looks different than success at 22.

It looks like options. Flexibility. Control over time. Health that allows you to enjoy life. Strong relationships. Purpose in what you do.

It looks like money working quietly in the background instead of creating constant stress. It looks like saying no without fear. It looks like not needing to impress anyone.

It looks like energy directed toward what matters most, not what looks best from the outside.

This version of success is harder to compare. That is why it is more meaningful.

Former athletes who thrive stop measuring themselves by others' highlight reels. They build lives that work for them, even if they look ordinary from the outside.

Building a New Scoreboard

You need a new scoreboard.

Not one built by social media, comparison, or outdated definitions of success. One built intentionally around what matters to you now.

That scoreboard might include financial stability. Time freedom. Physical and mental health. Meaningful relationships. Growth. Contribution. Peace of mind.

The metrics are personal. That is the point.

When you define your own scoreboard, decisions get easier. Spending aligns with priorities. Career choices make more sense. You stop chasing things that do not actually move your life forward.

Money becomes a tool instead of a measuring stick.

Athletes know how to train for defined goals. The challenge is choosing the right ones once the old scoreboard disappears.

Coach's Perspective: What Would Your Coach Say?

Your coach would refocus you.

They would say:

Define the goal.

Do not chase noise.

Measure what matters.

Control your effort.

Win your game.

Financially, that means aligning money with values instead of appearances. Building a life that works for you instead of performing for others.

Game Situations and Decision Points

Situation one. You feel behind because others look ahead.

Do you compare or refocus on your own scoreboard?

Situation two. A purchase boosts status but strains finances.

Do you chase image or alignment?

Situation three. A career move increases income but reduces fulfillment.

Do you accept automatically, or reassess what winning means for you?

Each decision shapes your version of winning.

Common Athlete Mistakes and Financial Parallels

Athletes chase comparison. Satisfaction disappears.

Athletes equate income with success. Fulfillment gets ignored.

Athletes follow external scoreboards. Misalignment grows.

Athletes delay reflection. Drift replaces intention.

Recognizing these patterns restores clarity and control.

Winning the Long Game

Winning after sports is not louder. It is quieter.

It is not measured in trophies. It is measured in alignment, stability, and freedom. It is measured in how your life feels, not how it looks.

When you define success intentionally, money supports life instead of driving it. Pressure drops. Confidence becomes internal instead of dependent on comparison.

That is real winning.

Athlete Takeaways

Status is a poor substitute for performance.

Income supports success but does not define it.

Comparison traps distort priorities.

Success in adulthood looks like alignment, not applause.

Build a personal scoreboard based on values and what actually matters to you.

Chapter 30: Staying Connected Without Living in the Past

Leaving sports does not just change what you do. It changes where you belong.

For years, your identity was reinforced daily. Teammates. Coaches. Locker rooms. Shared struggle. Built-in community. You knew where you fit and who you were connected to. You did not have to search for belonging. It was part of the environment.

When that ends, the silence can be heavy.

This chapter is about staying connected without getting stuck. Building community that moves you forward. Honoring the past without living in it. Creating an identity that grows instead of fading.

The Role of Community, Mentorship, and New Locker Rooms

Community does not disappear when sports end. It just stops being automatic.

Locker rooms are replaced by offices, homes, and screens. Mentorship becomes optional instead of assigned. Belonging has to be built intentionally rather than handed to you.

Former athletes often miss the daily camaraderie more than the competition. The shared effort. The jokes. The accountability. The feeling of being part of something bigger than yourself.

New locker rooms exist, but they do not look the same. Professional networks. Volunteer groups. Faith communities. Business partnerships. Alumni circles. Small peer groups. Fitness communities. These are places where shared effort and connection can grow again.

Mentorship becomes especially important. Learning from people a few steps ahead provides perspective and direction when structure is gone. Mentors normalize the transition, shorten learning curves, and remind you that uncertainty is part of growth.

Staying connected is not about replacing sports. It is about rebuilding belonging in a new form.

Why Isolation Hits Former Athletes Hard

Athletes are conditioned to be surrounded by people.

Training is collective. Travel is shared. Pressure is experienced together. Success and failure are processed as a group. Even tough days are rarely faced alone.

When that disappears, isolation feels sharper than it does for most people.

Many former athletes internalize this isolation as failure. They assume something is wrong with them because they feel disconnected. In reality, they lost a system that once met emotional and social needs automatically.

Isolation impacts more than mood. It affects decision-making, confidence, and motivation. Without regular conversation and perspective, doubts grow louder. Small problems feel bigger. Financial and career mistakes often follow isolation because there is no sounding board.

Connection is protective.

Athletes thrive in environments with shared accountability. Without it, drift accelerates and confidence erodes quietly.

Finding Purpose Without the Team

Purpose used to be defined externally.

Practice schedules. Games. Goals. Seasons. Purpose was assigned. You knew exactly what to work toward and when.

After sports, purpose must be chosen.

This is uncomfortable at first. It requires reflection instead of instruction. Many former athletes avoid this work and stay busy instead. Busyness feels like progress, but without direction it leads to frustration.

True purpose is not found in replicating sports. It is found in applying the same values to new arenas.

Leadership in the workplace. Teaching younger athletes. Building a business. Serving a community. Creating something meaningful. Competing in different ways.

Purpose evolves. It does not arrive fully formed. It develops through action, reflection, and adjustment.

Those who take time to explore it build more satisfying lives than those who cling to old identities or wait for clarity to appear on its own.

Healthy Nostalgia vs Being Stuck

Nostalgia is not the enemy.

Remembering good times, lessons learned, and relationships built is healthy. It provides context and gratitude. It honors effort and growth.

The problem arises when nostalgia becomes identity.

Living in the past prevents growth. Constantly reliving former glory limits future possibility. Measuring current life against peak athletic moments guarantees dissatisfaction because few experiences match that intensity.

Healthy nostalgia honors the past while allowing change.

Being stuck replays the past as proof that nothing else will compare. It turns memories into a ceiling instead of a foundation.

Former athletes who thrive respect who they were without letting it define who they must remain.

Creating a Forward-Looking Identity

Identity is not lost when sports end. It transitions.

The traits that made you successful did not disappear. Discipline. Resilience. Team-first mindset. Competitive drive. Ability to handle pressure. These qualities still exist. They just need new direction.

Creating a forward-looking identity means asking better questions.

Who am I becoming, not who was I.

What matters now, not what mattered then.

How do I use my experience to build something meaningful next.

This identity is active. It grows. It adapts. It makes room for new roles without erasing the old ones.

Former athletes who define themselves by what they are building instead of what they once were stay energized and connected. Growth replaces loss.

Coach's Perspective: What Would Your Coach Say?

Your coach would push you forward.

They would say:

Honor the work.

Keep growing.

Find your next challenge.

Do not live in the past.

Lead where you are.

Financially and personally, that means investing in relationships, purpose, and growth instead of clinging to old scoreboards or old definitions of success.

Game Situations and Decision Points

Situation one. You miss the locker room and daily camaraderie.

Do you isolate, or seek new community intentionally?

Situation two. Stories from the past dominate conversations.

Do you relive, or redirect toward what you are building now?

Situation three. Identity feels unclear.

Do you avoid the discomfort, or explore it intentionally?

Each choice shapes connection, confidence, and long-term fulfillment.

Common Athlete Mistakes and Financial Parallels

Athletes isolate instead of rebuilding community. Confidence drops and decisions suffer.

Athletes cling to old identity. Growth stalls.

Athletes avoid mentorship. Mistakes repeat that others could have helped prevent.

Athletes chase nostalgia. Purpose fades and motivation weakens.

Recognizing these patterns opens new paths instead of repeating old ones.

Winning the Long Game

Connection does not mean holding on.

It means evolving.

Former athletes who build new communities, find purpose beyond the team, and create forward-looking identities thrive long after sports end. They stay connected to their past while investing in their future.

The past will always be part of you. It just does not have to be the whole story.

Staying connected while moving forward is the real victory.

Athlete Takeaways

Community must be rebuilt intentionally after sports.

Isolation increases drift and mistakes.

Purpose evolves beyond the team.

Healthy nostalgia honors the past without trapping you in it.

Identity after sports is about who you are becoming, not only who you were.

Glossary of Soccer and Financial Terms

Asset Allocation

Financial Definition:

How money is divided among different investment types such as stocks, bonds, and cash to balance risk and return.

Soccer Comparison:

How responsibility, difficulty, and timing are distributed across the pitch. Too much focus on attack or defense without balance causes breakdowns.

Assets

Financial Definition:

Things you own that have value, such as cash, investments, real estate, or retirement accounts.

Soccer Comparison:

Your strengths as a player. Skills, conditioning, experience, and preparation that contribute to overall performance.

Bonds

Financial Definition:

Loans made to governments or companies that pay interest and return principal over time.

Soccer Comparison:

Midfield control. Not flashy, but essential for stability and tempo when pressure increases.

Budget

Financial Definition:

A plan for how income is allocated toward expenses, savings, and goals.

Soccer Comparison:

Match planning and substitutions. Without knowing timing and roles, execution breaks down.

Cash Flow

Financial Definition:

Money coming in versus money going out.

Soccer Comparison:

Energy management. Start too fast and you fade late. Manage it well and you finish strong.

Compounding

Financial Definition:

Earnings that generate additional earnings over time.

Soccer Comparison:

Daily touches and repetition. Each rep builds on the last and progress accelerates quietly.

Credit

Financial Definition:

The ability to borrow money with the promise of repayment.

Soccer Comparison:

Trust from the coach. Earned through consistency and discipline, lost quickly when misused.

Debt

Financial Definition:

Money borrowed that must be repaid, often with interest.

Soccer Comparison:

Extra weight in training. Manageable in small amounts, dangerous when excessive.

Diversification

Financial Definition:

Spreading investments across different assets to reduce risk.

Soccer Comparison:

Depth across positions. You do not rely on one player or one tactic to carry the season.

Emergency Fund

Financial Definition:

Savings set aside for unexpected expenses.

Soccer Comparison:

A reliable substitute on the bench. You hope you do not need it, but it saves matches when things go wrong.

ETF (Exchange-Traded Fund)

Financial Definition:

A fund that holds many investments and trades like a stock.

Soccer Comparison:

A well-drilled squad. Team-based execution instead of hero ball.

Fees / Expense Ratios

Financial Definition:

Costs associated with managing investments.

Soccer Comparison:

Poor spacing and sloppy transitions. Small leaks that quietly drain momentum over time.

Growth Investing

Financial Definition:

Investing in companies expected to grow faster than average.

Soccer Comparison:

High-press attacking play. More upside, but requires conditioning and discipline.

Insurance

Financial Definition:

Protection against financial loss from unexpected events.

Soccer Comparison:

Shin guards and proper boots. You do not play without protection when risk rises.

Liquidity

Financial Definition:

How easily money can be accessed without penalty or delay.

Soccer Comparison:

Tactical flexibility. The ability to adjust shape quickly when the match changes.

Net Worth

Financial Definition:

Assets minus liabilities.

Soccer Comparison:

The final scoreline over a season. Not one play, but the full outcome.

Rebalancing

Financial Definition:

Adjusting investments back to their intended mix over time.

Soccer Comparison:

Halftime adjustments that restore shape and control.

Risk

Financial Definition:

The chance that outcomes differ from expectations, including loss.

Soccer Comparison:

Difficulty selection. Higher reward requires accepting more risk.

Roth IRA

Financial Definition:

A retirement account where money grows tax-free if rules are followed.

Soccer Comparison:

Extra work in preseason so matches feel cleaner later.

Stocks

Financial Definition:

Ownership shares in a company.

Soccer Comparison:

Primary attackers. They drive scoring but need support to succeed.

Tax-Advantaged Accounts

Financial Definition:

Accounts that provide tax benefits, often with rules and restrictions.

Soccer Comparison:

Structured training environments. Rules exist to improve outcomes.

Volatility

Financial Definition:

Short-term ups and downs in market value.

Soccer Comparison:

Momentum swings. Normal movement that only becomes a problem if you panic.

Permanent Loss

Financial Definition:

Money that cannot recover due to poor decisions or panic.

Soccer Comparison:

Getting caught out of position. Usually caused by abandoning fundamentals.

Total Return

Financial Definition:

Investment return from both price growth and income.

Soccer Comparison:

The full match performance. Every phase matters, not just goals.

Value Investing

Financial Definition:

Investing in assets believed to be undervalued.

Soccer Comparison:

Clean, efficient play. Less flash, more control, consistent results.

Yield

Financial Definition:

Income generated from an investment.

Soccer Comparison:

Reliable goals from set pieces. Not dramatic, but dependable.

Final Note

This glossary reinforces one core principle:

Financial success, like success in **soccer**, comes from balance, discipline, timing, and repetition.

That philosophy runs through **Soccer Money 101** and carries forward long after competition ends.

Disclaimers

Soccer Money 101

Educational Purpose Only

This book is for educational purposes only.

The information provided in **Soccer Money 101** is intended to help readers understand general financial concepts using soccer-based analogies. It is not individualized financial, investment, tax, legal, or insurance advice.

Every financial situation is different. Your goals, income, family circumstances, risk tolerance, and time horizon are unique. What works for one person may not be appropriate for another.

Not Financial, Investment, or Legal Advice

Nothing in this book should be interpreted as a recommendation to buy, sell, or hold any specific investment, financial product, or strategy.

This book does not replace advice from qualified professionals, including but not limited to:

- Financial advisors
- Accountants or tax professionals
- Attorneys
- Insurance professionals

Before making financial decisions, readers should consult professionals who can evaluate their individual situation.

No Guarantees or Promises of Results

All investing involves risk, including the possible loss of principal.

Past performance does not guarantee future results. Markets fluctuate. Economic conditions change. Outcomes cannot be predicted or guaranteed.

The examples and scenarios in this book are illustrative only and may not reflect actual results or real-world outcomes.

Tax and Legal Information

Any discussion of taxes, retirement accounts, estate planning, or legal structures is general in nature.

Tax laws and regulations change frequently and vary by jurisdiction. Legal requirements differ based on location and personal circumstances.

Readers should seek personalized tax or legal advice before acting on any information related to these topics.

Athlete and Career Considerations

This book discusses financial topics as they relate to athletes and former athletes, including career transitions and income changes.

It does not provide career placement services, employment advice, or guarantees related to income, compensation, or career success.

Use of Analogies

Soccer and sports analogies are used to make financial concepts easier to understand.

These analogies are educational tools only and should not be interpreted literally. Financial decisions require analysis beyond analogy.

Personal Responsibility

By reading this book, you acknowledge that:

- You are responsible for your own financial decisions
- You understand that financial outcomes involve uncertainty
- You agree to seek appropriate professional guidance when needed

Education improves decision-making, but responsibility remains with the individual.

Contact Information

If you would like to learn more about the concepts discussed in this book or explore additional educational resources, Pat Brown can be found through public platforms including LinkedIn, Twitter, and via Google search.

For questions specifically related to **Soccer Money 101**, you may contact Pat Brown at:

info@soccermoney101.com

Final Reminder

Financial success is built over time through discipline, planning, and consistency.

This book provides a framework, not a guarantee.

Use it as a guide, not a substitute for professional advice.

Pat Brown OLB, University of Kansas

Made in the USA
Monee, IL
04 November 2026

67387589R00115